UNIVERSITY CASEBOOK SERIES®

2023 STATUTORY APPENDIX AND CASE SUPPLEMENT TO

COX, BOK & GORMAN'S

LABOR LAW

CASES AND MATERIALS

SEVENTEENTH EDITION

MATTHEW W. FINKIN
Swanlund Chair and Center for Advanced Study Professor of Law
University of Illinois

TIMOTHY P. GLYNN
Andrea J. Catania Endowed Professor of Law
Seton Hall University School of Law

860 Blue Gentian Road, Suite 350
Eagan, MN 55121
1-877-888-1330

Printed in the United States of America

ISBN: 978-1-68561-999-2

TABLE OF CONTENTS

TABLE OF CASES

The principal cases are in bold type.

UNIVERSITY CASEBOOK SERIES®

2023 STATUTORY APPENDIX AND CASE SUPPLEMENT TO

COX, BOK & GORMAN'S

LABOR LAW

CASES AND MATERIALS

SEVENTEENTH EDITION

SHERMAN ACT

26 Stat. 209 (1890), as amended, 15 U.S.C. §§ 1 et seq. (1988).

Sec. 1. Every contract, combination in the form of a trust or otherwise, or conspiracy, in restraint of trade or commerce among the several States, or with foreign nations, is hereby declared to be illegal. Every person who shall make any such contract or engage in any such combination or conspiracy, shall be deemed guilty of a misdemeanor, and, on conviction thereof, shall be punished by fine not exceeding five thousand dollars, or by imprisonment not exceeding one year, or by both said punishments, in the discretion of the court.

Sec. 2. Every person who shall monopolize, or attempt to monopolize, or combine or conspire with any other person or persons, to monopolize any part of the trade or commerce among the several States, or with foreign nations, shall be deemed guilty of a misdemeanor, and, on conviction thereof, shall be punished by fine not exceeding five thousand dollars, or by imprisonment not exceeding one year, or by both said punishments, in the discretion of the court.

Sec. 3. Every contract, combination in form of trust or otherwise, or conspiracy, in restraint of trade or commerce in any territory of the United States or of the District of Columbia, or in restraint of trade or commerce between any such territory and another, or between any such territory or territories and any State or States or the District of Columbia, or with foreign nations, or between the District of Columbia and any State or States or foreign nations, is hereby declared illegal. Every person who shall make any such contract or engage in any such combination or conspiracy, shall be deemed guilty of a misdemeanor, and, on conviction thereof, shall be punished by fine not exceeding five thousand dollars, or by imprisonment not exceeding one year, or by both said punishments, in the discretion of the court.

Sec. 4. The several circuit courts of the United States are hereby invested with jurisdiction to prevent and restrain violations of this act; and it shall be the duty of the several district attorneys of the United States, in their respective districts, under the direction of the Attorney General, to institute proceedings in equity to prevent and restrain such violations. Such proceedings may be by way of petition setting forth the case and praying that such violation shall be enjoined or otherwise prohibited. When the parties complained of shall have been duly notified of such petition the court shall proceed, as soon as may be, to the hearing and determination of the case; and pending such petition and before final decree, the court may at any time make such temporary restraining order or prohibition as shall be deemed just in the premises.

Sec. 5. Whenever it shall appear to the court before which any proceeding under section 4 of this act may be pending, that the ends of justice require that other parties should be brought before the court, the court may cause them to be summoned, whether they reside in the district in which the court is held or not; and subpoenas to that end may be served in any district by the marshal thereof.

Sec. 6. Any property owned under any contract or by any combination, or pursuant to any conspiracy (and being the subject thereof) mentioned in section 1 of this act, and being in the course of transportation from one State to another, or to a foreign country, shall be forfeited to the United States, and may be seized and condemned by like proceedings as those provided by law for the forfeiture, seizure, and condemnation of property imported into the United States contrary to law.

Sec. 7. Any person who shall be injured in his business or property by any other person or corporation by reason of anything forbidden or declared to be unlawful by this act, may sue therefor in any Circuit Court of the United States in the district in which the defendant resides or is found, without respect to the amount in controversy, and shall recover three-fold the damages sustained, and the costs of suit, including a reasonable attorney's fee.

Sec. 8. That the word "person," or "persons" wherever used in this act shall be deemed to include corporations and associations existing under or authorized by the laws of either the United States, the laws of any State or the laws of any foreign country.

CLAYTON ACT

38 Stat. 730 (1914), as amended, 15 U.S.C. §§ 12 et seq. (1988).

Be it enacted by the Senate and House of Representatives of the United States of America in Congress assembled, That "anti-trust laws," as used herein, includes the Act entitled "An Act to protect trade and commerce against unlawful restraints and monopolies", approved July second, eighteen hundred and ninety [Sherman Act, supra.] * * *

* * *

Sec. 6. That the labor of a human being is not a commodity or article of commerce. Nothing contained in the anti-trust laws shall be construed to forbid the existence and operation of labor, agricultural, or horticultural organizations, instituted for the purposes of mutual help, and not having capital stock or conducted for profit, or to forbid or restrain individual members of such organizations from lawfully carrying out the legitimate objects thereof; nor shall such organizations, or the members thereof, be held or construed to be illegal combinations or conspiracies in restraint of trade, under the anti-trust laws.

* * *

Sec. 16. That any person, firm, corporation, or association shall be entitled to sue for and have injunctive relief, in any court of the United States having jurisdiction over the parties, against threatened loss or damage by a violation of the anti-trust laws, including sections two, three, seven and eight of this Act, when and under the same conditions and principles as injunctive relief against threatened conduct that will cause loss or damage is granted by courts of equity, under the rules governing such proceedings, and upon the execution of proper bond against damages for an injunction improvidently granted and a showing that the danger of irreparable loss or damage is immediate, a preliminary injunction may issue: *Provided,* That nothing herein contained shall be construed to entitle any person, firm, corporation, or association, except the United States, to bring suit in equity for injunctive relief against any common carrier subject to the provisions of the Act to regulate commerce, approved February fourth, eighteen hundred and eighty-seven, in respect of any matter subject to the regulation, supervision, or other jurisdiction of the Interstate Commerce Commission.

* * *

Sec. 20. That no restraining order or injunction shall be granted by any court of the United States, or a judge or the judges thereof, in any case between an employer and employees, or between employers and employees, or between employees, or between persons employed and persons seeking employment, involving, or growing out of, a dispute concerning terms or conditions of employment, unless necessary to prevent irreparable injury to property, or to a property right, of the party making the application, for which injury there is no adequate remedy at law, and such property or property right must be described with particularity in the application, which must be in writing and sworn to by the applicant or by his agent or attorney.

And no such restraining order or injunction shall prohibit any person or persons, whether singly or in concert, from terminating any relation of employment, or from ceasing to perform any work or labor, or from recommending, advising, or persuading others by peaceful means so to do; or from attending at any place where any such person or persons may lawfully be, for the purpose of peacefully obtaining or communicating information, or from peacefully persuading any person to work or to abstain from working; or from ceasing to patronize or to employ any party to such dispute, or from recommending, advising, or persuading others by peaceful and lawful means so to do; or from paying or giving to, or withholding from, any person engaged in such dispute, any strike benefits or other moneys or things of value; or from peaceably assembling in a lawful manner, and for lawful purposes; or from doing any act or thing which might lawfully be done in the absence of such dispute by any party thereto; nor shall any of the acts specified in this paragraph be considered or held to be violations of any law of the United States.

* * *

Norris-LaGuardia Act

47 Stat. 70 (1932), 29 U.S.C. §§ 101–15 (1988).

Sec. 1. No court of the United States, as herein defined, shall have jurisdiction to issue any restraining order or temporary or permanent injunction in a case involving or growing out of a labor dispute, except in a strict conformity with the provisions of this Act; nor shall any such restraining order or temporary or permanent injunction be issued contrary to the public policy declared in this Act.

Sec. 2. In the interpretation of this Act and in determining the jurisdiction and authority of the courts of the United States, as such jurisdiction and authority are herein defined and limited, the public policy of the United States is hereby declared as follows:

Whereas under prevailing economic conditions, developed with the aid of governmental authority for owners of property to organize in the corporate and other forms of ownership association, the individual unorganized worker is commonly helpless to exercise actual liberty of contract and to protect his freedom of labor, and thereby to obtain acceptable terms and conditions of employment, wherefore, though he should be free to decline to associate with his fellows, it is necessary that he have full freedom of association, self-organization, and designation of representatives of his own choosing, to negotiate the terms and conditions of his employment, and that he shall be free from the interference, restraint, or coercion of employers of labor, or their agents, in the designation of such representatives or in self-organization or in other concerted activities for the purpose of collective bargaining or other mutual aid or protection; therefore, the following definitions of, and limitations upon, the jurisdiction and authority of the courts of the United States are hereby enacted.

Sec. 3. Any undertaking or promise, such as is described in this section, or any other undertaking or promise in conflict with the public policy declared in section 2 of this Act, is hereby declared to be contrary to the public policy of the United States, shall not be enforceable in any court of the United States and shall not afford any basis for the granting of legal or equitable relief by any such court, including specifically the following:

Every undertaking or promise hereafter made, whether written or oral, express or implied, constituting or contained in any contract or agreement of hiring or employment between any individual, firm, company, association, or corporation, and any employee or prospective employee of the same whereby

(a) Either party to such contract or agreement undertakes or promises not to join, become, or remain a member of any labor organization or of any employer organization; or

(b) Either party to such contract or agreement undertakes or promises that he will withdraw from an employment relation in the event that he joins, becomes, or remains a member of any labor organization or of any employer organization.

Sec. 4. No court of the United States shall have jurisdiction to issue any restraining order or temporary or permanent injunction in any case involving or growing out of any labor dispute to prohibit any person or persons participating or interested in such dispute (as these terms are herein defined) from doing, whether singly or in concert, any of the following acts:

(a) Ceasing or refusing to perform any work or to remain in any relation of employment;

(b) Becoming or remaining a member of any labor organization or of any employer organization, regardless of any such undertaking or promise as is described in section 3 of this Act;

(c) Paying or giving to, or withholding from, any person participating or interested in such labor dispute, any strike or unemployment benefits or insurance, or other moneys or things of value;

(d) By all lawful means aiding any person participating or interested in any labor dispute who is being proceeded against in, or is prosecuting, any action or suit in any court of the United States or of any State;

(e) Giving publicity to the existence of, or the facts involved in, any labor dispute, whether by advertising, speaking, patrolling, or by any other method not involving fraud or violence;

(f) Assembling peaceably to act or to organize to act in promotion of their interests in a labor dispute;

(g) Advising or notifying any person of an intention to do any of the Acts heretofore specified;

(h) Agreeing with other persons to do or not to do any of the acts heretofore specified; and

(i) Advising, urging, or otherwise causing or inducing without fraud or violence the acts heretofore specified, regardless of any such undertaking or promise as is described in section 3 of this Act.

Sec. 5. No court of the United States shall have jurisdiction to issue a restraining order or temporary or permanent injunction upon the ground that any of the persons participating or interested in a labor dispute constitute or are engaged in an unlawful combination or conspiracy because of the doing in concert of the acts enumerated in section 4 of this Act.

Sec. 6. No officer or member of any association or organization, and no association or organization participating or interested in a labor dispute, shall be held responsible or liable in any court of the United

States for the unlawful acts of individual officers, members, or agents, except upon clear proof of actual participation in, or actual authorization of, such acts, or of ratification of such acts after actual knowledge thereof.

Sec. 7. No court of the United States shall have jurisdiction to issue a temporary or permanent injunction in any case involving or growing out of a labor dispute, as herein defined, except after hearing the testimony of witnesses in open court (with opportunity for cross-examination) in support of the allegations of a complaint made under oath, and testimony in opposition thereto, if offered, and except after findings of fact by the court, to the effect—

(a) That unlawful acts have been threatened and will be committed unless restrained or have been committed and will be continued unless restrained, but no injunction or temporary restraining order shall be issued on account of any threat or unlawful act excepting against the person or persons, association, or organization making the threat or committing the unlawful act or actually authorizing or ratifying the same after actual knowledge thereof;

(b) That substantial and irreparable injury to complainant's property will follow:

(c) That as to each item of relief granted greater injury will be inflicted upon complainant by the denial of relief than will be inflicted upon defendants by the granting of relief;

(d) That complainant has no adequate remedy at law; and

(e) That the public officers charged with the duty to protect complainant's property are unable or unwilling to furnish adequate protection.

Such hearing shall be held after due and personal notice thereof has been given, in such manner as the court shall direct, to all known persons against whom relief is sought, and also to the chief of those public officials of the county and city within which the unlawful acts have been threatened or committed charged with the duty to protect complainant's property: *Provided, however*, That if a complainant shall also allege that, unless a temporary restraining order shall be issued without notice, a substantial and irreparable injury to complainant's property will be unavoidable, such a temporary restraining order may be issued upon testimony under oath, sufficient, if sustained, to justify the court in issuing a temporary injunction upon a hearing after notice. Such a temporary restraining order shall be effective for no longer than five days and shall become void at the expiration of said five days. No temporary restraining order or temporary injunction shall be issued except on condition that complainant shall first file an undertaking with adequate security in an amount to be fixed by the court sufficient to recompense those enjoined for any loss, expense, or damage caused by the improvident or erroneous issuance of such order or injunction, including all reasonable costs (together with a reasonable attorney's fee) and expense of defense against the order or against the granting of any injunctive relief sought in the same proceeding and subsequently denied by the court.

The undertaking herein mentioned shall be understood to signify an agreement entered into by the complainant and the surety upon which a decree may be rendered in the same suit or proceeding against said complainant and surety, upon a hearing to assess damages of which hearing complainant and surety shall have reasonable notice, the said complainant and surety submitting themselves to the jurisdiction of the court for that purpose. But nothing herein contained shall deprive any party having a claim or cause of action under or upon such undertaking from electing to pursue his ordinary remedy by suit at law or in equity.

Sec. 8. No restraining order or injunctive relief shall be granted to any complainant who has failed to comply with any obligation imposed by law which is involved in the labor dispute in question, or who has failed to make every reasonable effort to settle such dispute either by negotiation or with the aid of any available governmental machinery of mediation or voluntary arbitration.

Sec. 9. No restraining order or temporary or permanent injunction shall be granted in a case involving or growing out of a labor dispute, except on the basis of findings of fact made and filed by the court in the record of the case prior to the issuance of such restraining order or injunction; and every restraining order or injunction granted in a case involving or growing out of a labor dispute shall include only a prohibition of such specific act or acts as may be expressly complained of in the bill of complaint or petition filed in such case and as shall be expressly included in said findings of fact made and filed by the court as provided herein.

Sec. 10. Whenever any court of the United States shall issue or deny any temporary injunction in a case involving or growing out of a labor dispute, the court shall, upon the request of any party to the proceedings and on his filing the usual bond for costs, forthwith certify as in ordinary cases the record of the case to the circuit court of appeals for its review. Upon the filing of such record in the circuit court of appeals, the appeal shall be heard and the temporary injunctive order affirmed, modified, or set aside with the greatest possible expedition, giving the proceedings precedence over all other matters except older matters of the same character.

Sec. 11.* In all cases arising under this Act in which a person shall be charged with contempt in a court of the United States (as herein defined), the accused shall enjoy the right to a speedy and public trial by an impartial jury of the State and district wherein the contempt shall

* Sections 11 and 12 were repealed in 1948, 62 Stat. 862. The text of Section 11 is now in 18 U.S.C. § 3692 (1982); Rule 42 of the Federal Rules of Criminal Procedure now governs the matters formerly treated in Section 12.

have been committed: *Provided*, That this right shall not apply to contempts committed in the presence of the court or so near thereto as to interfere directly with the administration of justice or to apply to the misbehavior, misconduct, or disobedience of any officer of the court in respect to the writs, orders, or process of the court.

Sec. 12.* The defendant in any proceeding for contempt of court may file with the court a demand for the retirement of the judge sitting in the proceeding, if the contempt arises from an attack upon the character or conduct of such judge and if the attack occurred elsewhere than in the presence of the court or so near thereto as to interfere directly with the administration of justice. Upon the filing of any such demand the judge shall thereupon proceed no further, but another judge shall be designated in the same manner as is provided by law. The demand shall be filed prior to the hearing in the contempt proceeding.

Sec. 13. When used in this Act, and for the purposes of this Act—

(a) A case shall be held to involve or to grow out of a labor dispute when the case involves persons who are engaged in the same industry, trade, craft, or occupation; or have direct or indirect interests therein; or who are employees of the same employer; or who are members of the same or an affiliated organization of employers or employees; whether such dispute is (1) between one or more employers or associations of employers and one or more employees or associations of employees; (2) between one or more employers or associations of employers and one or more employers or associations of employers; or (3) between one or more employees or associations of employees and one or more employees or associations of employees; or when the case involves any conflicting or competing interests in a "labor dispute" (as hereinafter defined) of "persons participating or interested" therein (as hereinafter defined).

(b) A person or association shall be held to be a person participating or interested in a labor dispute if relief is sought against him or it, and if he or it is engaged in the same industry, trade, craft, or occupation in which such dispute occurs, or has a direct or indirect interest therein, or is a member, officer, or agent of any association composed in whole or in part of employers or employees engaged in such industry, trade, craft, or occupation.

(c) The term "labor dispute" includes any controversy concerning terms or conditions of employment, or concerning the association or representation of persons in negotiating, fixing, maintaining, changing, or seeking to arrange terms or conditions of employment, regardless of whether or not the disputants stand in the proximate relation of employer and employee.

(d) The term "court of the United States" means any court of the United States whose jurisdiction has been or may be conferred or defined or limited by Act of Congress, including the courts of the District of Columbia.

Sec. 14. If any provision of this Act or the application thereof to any person or circumstance is held unconstitutional or otherwise invalid, the remaining provisions of the Act and the application of such provisions to other persons or circumstances shall not be affected thereby.

Sec. 15. All Acts and parts of Acts in conflict with the provisions of this Act are hereby repealed.

RAILWAY LABOR ACT

44 Stat., Part II, 577 (1926), as amended;
45 U.S.C. §§ 151–88 (1988).

TITLE I

Sec. 1. When used in this Act and for the purposes of this Act—

First. The term "carrier" includes any express company, sleeping-car company, carrier by railroad, subject to the Interstate Commerce Act, and any company which is directly or indirectly owned or controlled by or under common control with any carrier by railroad and which operates any equipment or facilities or performs any service (other than trucking service) in connection with the transportation, receipt, delivery, elevation, transfer in transit, refrigeration or icing, storage, and handling of property transported by railroad, and any receiver, trustee, or other individual or body, judicial or otherwise, when in the possession of the business of any such "carrier": *Provided, however,* That the term "carrier" shall not include any street, interurban, or suburban electric railway, unless such railway is operating as a part of a general steam-railroad system of transportation, but shall not exclude any part of the general steam-railroad system of transportation now or hereafter operated by any other motive power. The Interstate Commerce Commission is authorized and directed upon request of the Mediation Board or upon complaint of any party interested to determine after hearing whether any line operated by electric power falls within the terms of this proviso. The term "carrier" shall not include any company by reason of its being engaged in the mining of coal, the supplying of coal to a carrier where delivery is not beyond the mine tipple, and the operation of equipment or facilities therefor, or in any of such activities.

Second. The term "Adjustment Board" means the National Railroad Adjustment Board created by this Act.

Third. The term "Mediation Board" means the National Mediation Board created by this Act.

Fourth. The term "commerce" means commerce among the several States or between any State, Territory, or the District of Columbia and any foreign nation, or between any Territory or the District of Columbia and any State, or between any Territory and any other Territory, or between any Territory and the District of Columbia, or within any Territory or the District of Columbia, or between points in the same State but through any other State or any Territory or the District of Columbia or any foreign nation.

Fifth. The term "employee" as used herein includes every person in the service of a carrier (subject to its continuing authority to supervise and direct the manner of rendition of his service) who performs any work defined as that of an employee or subordinate official in the orders of the

Interstate Commerce Commission now in effect, and as the same may be amended or interpreted by orders hereafter entered by the Commission pursuant to the authority which is conferred upon it to enter orders amending or interpreting such existing orders: *Provided, however,* That no occupational classification made by order of the Interstate Commerce Commission shall be construed to define the crafts according to which railway employees may be organized by their voluntary action, nor shall the jurisdiction or powers of such employee organizations be regarded as in any way limited or defined by the provisions of this Act or by the orders of the Commission. The term "employee" shall not include any individual while such individual is engaged in the physical operations consisting of the mining of coal, the preparation of coal, the handling (other than movement by rail with standard railroad locomotives) of coal not beyond the mine tipple, or the loading of coal at the tipple.

Sixth. The term "representative" means any person or persons, labor union, organization, or corporation designated either by a carrier or group of carriers or by its or their employees, to act for it or them.

Seventh. The term "district court" includes the United States District Court for the District of Columbia; and the term "circuit court of appeals" includes the United States Court of Appeals for the District of Columbia.

This Act may be cited as the "Railway Labor Act."

Sec. 2. The purposes of the Act are:

(1) To avoid any interruption to commerce or to the operation of any carrier engaged therein; (2) to forbid any limitation upon freedom of association among employees or any denial, as a condition of employment or otherwise, of the right of employees to join a labor organization; (3) to provide for the complete independence of carriers and of employees in the matter of self-organization; (4) to provide for the prompt and orderly settlement of all disputes concerning rates of pay, rules, or working conditions; (5) to provide for the prompt and orderly settlement of all disputes growing out of grievances or out of the interpretation or application of agreements covering rates of pay, rules, or working conditions.

First. It shall be the duty of all carriers, their officers, agents, and employees to exert every reasonable effort to make and maintain agreements concerning rates of pay, rules, and working conditions, and to settle all disputes, whether arising out of the application of such agreements or otherwise, in order to avoid any interruption to commerce or to the operation of any carrier growing out of any dispute between the carrier and the employees thereof.

Second. All disputes between a carrier or carriers and its or their employees shall be considered, and, if possible, decided, with all expedition, in conference between representatives designated and authorized so to confer, respectively, by the carrier or carriers and by the employees thereof interested in the dispute.

Third. Representatives, for the purposes of this Act, shall be designated by the respective parties without interference, influence, or coercion by either party over the designation of representatives by the other; and neither party shall in any way interfere with, influence, or coerce the other in its choice of representatives. Representatives of employees for the purposes of this Act need not be persons in the employ of the carrier, and no carrier shall, by interference, influence, or coercion seek in any manner to prevent the designation by its employees as their representatives of those who or which are not employees of the carrier.

Fourth. Employees shall have the right to organize and bargain collectively through representatives of their own choosing. The majority of any craft or class of employees shall have the right to determine who shall be the representative of the craft or class for the purposes of this Act. No carrier, its officers or agents, shall deny or in any way question the right of its employees to join, organize, or assist in organizing the labor organization of their choice, and it shall be unlawful for any carrier to interfere in any way with the organization of its employees, or to use the funds of the carrier in maintaining or assisting or contributing to any labor organization, labor representative, or other agency of collective bargaining, or in performing any work therefor, or to influence or coerce employees in an effort to induce them to join or remain or not to join or remain members of any labor organization or to deduct from the wages of employees any dues, fees, assessments, or other contributions payable to labor organizations, or to collect or to assist in the collection of any such dues, fees, assessments, or other contributions: *Provided*, That nothing in this Act shall be construed to prohibit a carrier from permitting an employee, individually, or local representatives of employees from conferring with management during working hours without loss of time, or to prohibit a carrier from furnishing free transportation to its employees while engaged in the business of a labor organization.

Fifth. No carrier, its officers, or agents shall require any person seeking employment to sign any contract or agreement promising to join or not to join a labor organization; and if any such contract has been enforced prior to the effective date of this Act, then such carrier shall notify the employees by an appropriate order that such contract has been discarded and is no longer binding on them in any way.

Sixth. In case of a dispute between a carrier or carriers and its or their employees, arising out of grievances or out of the interpretation or application of agreements concerning rates of pay, rules, or working conditions, it shall be the duty of the designated representative or representatives of such carrier or carriers and of such employees, within ten days after the receipt of notice of a desire on the part of either party to confer in respect to such dispute, to specify a time and place at which such conference shall be held: *Provided,* (1) That the place so specified shall be situated upon the line of the carrier involved or as otherwise mutually agreed upon; and (2) that the time so specified shall allow the designated conferees reasonable opportunity to reach such place of conference, but shall not exceed twenty days from the receipt of such notice: *And provided further,* That nothing in this Act shall be construed to supersede the provisions of any agreement (as to conferences) then in effect between the parties.

Seventh. No carrier, its officers, or agents shall change the rates of pay, rules, or working conditions of its employees, as a class as embodied in agreements except in the manner prescribed in such agreements or in section 6 of this Act.

Eighth. Every carrier shall notify its employees by printed notices in such form and posted at such times and places as shall be specified by the Mediation Board that all disputes between the carrier and its employees will be handled in accordance with the requirements of this Act, and in such notices there shall be printed verbatim, in large type, the third, fourth, and fifth paragraphs of this section. The provisions of said paragraphs are hereby made a part of the contract of employment between the carrier and each employee, and shall be held binding upon the parties, regardless of any other express or implied agreements between them.

Ninth. If any dispute shall arise among a carrier's employees as to who are the representatives of such employees designated and authorized in accordance with the requirements of this Act, it shall be the duty of the Mediation Board, upon request of either party to the dispute, to investigate such dispute and to certify to both parties, in writing, within thirty days after the receipt of the invocation of its services, the name or names of the individuals or organizations that have been designated and authorized to represent the employees involved in the dispute, and certify the same to the carrier. Upon receipt of such certification the carrier shall treat with the representative so certified as the representative of the craft or class for the purposes of this Act. In such an investigation, the Mediation Board shall be authorized to take a secret ballot of the employees involved, or to utilize any other appropriate method of ascertaining the names of their duly designated and authorized representatives in such manner as shall insure the choice of representatives by the employees without interference, influence, or coercion exercised by the carrier. In the conduct of any election for the purposes herein indicated the Board shall designate who may participate in the election and establish the rules to govern the election, or may appoint a committee of three neutral persons who after hearing shall within ten days designate the employees who may participate in the election. The Board shall have access to and have power to make copies of the books and records of the carriers to obtain and utilize such information as may be deemed necessary by it to carry out the purposes and provisions of this paragraph.

Tenth. The willful failure or refusal of any carrier, its officers, or agents to comply with the terms of the third, fourth, fifth, seventh, or eighth paragraph of this section shall be a misdemeanor, and upon conviction thereof the carrier, officer, or agent offending shall be subject to a fine of not less than $1,000 nor more than $20,000 or imprisonment for not more than six months, or both fine and imprisonment, for each offense, and each day during which such carrier, officer, or agent shall willfully fail or refuse to comply with the terms of the said paragraphs of this section shall constitute a separate offense. It shall be the duty of any United States attorney to whom any duly designated representative of a carrier's employees may apply to institute in the proper court and to prosecute under the direction of the Attorney General of the United States, all necessary proceedings for the enforcement of the provisions of this section, and for the punishment of all violations thereof and the costs and expenses of such prosecution shall be paid out of the appropriation for the expenses of the courts of the United States: *Provided,* That nothing in this Act shall be construed to require an individual employee to render labor or service without his consent, nor shall anything in this Act be construed to make the quitting of his labor by an individual employee an illegal act; nor shall any court issue any process to compel the performance by an individual employee of such labor or service, without his consent.

Eleventh. Notwithstanding any other provisions of this chapter, or of any other statute or law of the United States, or Territory thereof, or of any State, any carrier or carriers as defined in this chapter and a labor organization or labor organizations duly designated and authorized to represent employees in accordance with the requirements of this chapter shall be permitted—

(a) to make agreements, requiring, as a condition of continued employment, that within sixty days following the beginning of such employment, or the effective date of such agreements, whichever is the later, all employees shall become members of the labor organization representing their craft or class: *Provided,* That no such agreement shall require such condition of employment with respect to employees to whom membership is not available upon the same terms and conditions as are generally applicable to any other member or with respect to employees to whom membership was denied or terminated for any reason other than the failure of the employee to tender the periodic dues, initiation fees, and assessments (not including fines and penalties) uniformly required as a condition of acquiring or retaining membership.

(b) to make agreements providing for the deduction by such carrier or carriers from the wages of its or their employees in a craft or class and payment to the labor organization representing the craft or class of such employees, of any periodic dues, initiation fees, and assessments (not including fines and penalties) uniformly required as a condition of acquiring or retaining membership: *Provided*, That no such agreement shall be effective with respect to any individual employee until he shall have furnished the employer with a written assignment to the labor organization of such membership dues, initiation fees, and assessments, which shall be revocable in writing after the expiration of one year or upon the termination date of the applicable collective agreement, whichever occurs sooner.

* * *

Sec. 3. First. There is hereby established a Board, to be known as the "National Railroad Adjustment Board", the members of which shall be selected within thirty days after June 21, 1934, and it is hereby provided—

(a) That the said Adjustment Board shall consist of thirty-four members, seventeen of whom shall be selected by the carriers and seventeen by such labor organizations of the employees, national in scope, as have been or may be organized in accordance with the provisions of section 2 of this Act.

(b) The carriers, acting each through its board of directors or its receiver or receivers, trustee or trustees, or through an officer or officers designated for that purpose by such board, trustee or trustees, or receiver or receivers, shall prescribe the rules under which its representatives shall be selected and shall select the representatives of the carriers on the Adjustment Board and designate the division on which each such representative shall serve, but no carrier or system of carriers shall have more than one voting representative on any division of the Board.

(c) Except as provided in the second paragraph of subsection (h) of this section, the national labor organizations as defined in paragraph (a) of this section, acting each through the chief executive or other medium designated by the organization or association thereof, shall prescribe the rules under which the labor members of the Adjustment Board shall be selected and shall select such members and designate the division on which each member shall serve; but no labor organization shall have more than one voting representative on any division of the Board.

* * *

(h) The said Adjustment Board shall be composed of four divisions, whose proceedings shall be independent of one another, and the said divisions as well as the number of their members shall be as follows:

First division: To have jurisdiction over disputes involving train- and yard-service employees of carriers; that is, engineers, firemen, hostlers, and outside hostler helpers, conductors, trainmen, and yard-service employees. This division shall consist of eight members, four of whom shall be selected and designated by the carriers and four of whom shall be selected and designated by the labor organizations * * *.

Second division: To have jurisdiction over disputes involving machinists, boilermakers, blacksmiths, sheet-metal workers, electrical workers, car men, the helpers and apprentices of all the foregoing, coach cleaners, power-house employees, and railroad-shop laborers. This division shall consist of ten members, five of whom shall be selected by the carriers and five by the national labor organizations of the employees.

Third division: To have jurisdiction over disputes involving station, tower, and telegraph employees, train dispatchers, maintenance-of-way men, clerical employees, freight handlers, express, station, and store employees, signal men, sleeping-car conductors, sleeping-car porters, and maids and dining-car employees. This division shall consist of ten members, five of whom shall be selected by the carriers and five by the national labor organizations of employees.

Fourth division: To have jurisdiction over disputes involving employees of carriers directly or indirectly engaged in transportation of passengers or property by water, and all other employees of carriers over which jurisdiction is not given to the first, second, and third divisions. This division shall consist of six members, three of whom shall be selected by the carriers and three by the national labor organizations of the employees.

(i) The disputes between an employee or group of employees and a carrier or carriers growing out of grievances or out of the interpretation or application of agreements concerning rates of pay, rules, or working conditions, including cases pending and unadjusted on the date of approval of this Act, shall be handled in the usual manner up to and including the chief operating officer of the carrier designated to handle such disputes; but, failing to reach an adjustment in this manner, the disputes may be referred by petition of the parties or by either party to the appropriate division of the Adjustment Board with a full statement of the facts and all supporting data bearing upon the disputes.

(j) Parties may be heard either in person, by counsel, or by other representatives, as they may respectively elect, and the several divisions of the Adjustment Board shall give due notice of all hearings to the employee or employees and the carrier or carriers involved in any disputes submitted to them.

(k) Any division of the Adjustment Board shall have authority to empower two or more of its members to conduct hearings and make findings upon disputes, when properly submitted, at any place designated by the division: *Provided, however,* That except as provided in paragraph (h) of this section, final awards as to any such dispute must be made by the entire division as hereinafter provided.

* * *

(m) The awards of the several divisions of the Adjustment Board shall be stated in writing. A copy of the awards shall be furnished to the respective parties to the controversy, and the awards shall be final and binding upon both parties to the dispute. In case a dispute arises involving an interpretation of the award the division of the Board upon request of either party shall interpret the award in the light of the dispute.

(n) A majority vote of all members of the division of the Adjustment Board eligible to vote shall be competent to make an award with respect to any dispute submitted to it.

(*o*) In case of an award by any division of the Adjustment Board in favor of petitioner, the division of the Board shall make an order, directed to the carrier, to make the award effective and, if the award includes a requirement for the payment of money, to pay the employee the sum to which he is entitled under the award on or before a day named. In the event any division determines that an award favorable to the petitioner should not be made in any dispute referred to it, the division shall make an order to the petitioner stating such determination.

(p) If a carrier does not comply with an order of a division of the Adjustment Board within the time limit in such order, the petitioner, or any person for whose benefit such order was made, may file in the District Court of the United States for the district in which he resides or in which is located the principal operating office of the carrier, or through which the carrier operates, a petition setting forth briefly the causes for which he claims relief, and the order of the division of the Adjustment Board in the premises. Such suit in the District Court of the United States shall proceed in all respects as other civil suits, except that on the trial of such suit the findings and order of the division of the Adjustment Board shall be conclusive on the parties, and except that the petitioner shall not be liable for costs in the district court nor for costs at any subsequent stage of the proceedings, unless they accrue upon his appeal, and such costs shall be paid out of the appropriation for the expenses of the courts of the United States. If the petitioner shall finally prevail he shall be allowed a reasonable attorney's fee, to be taxed and collected as a part of the costs of the suit. The district courts are empowered, under the rules of the court governing actions at law, to make such order and enter such judgment, by writ of mandamus or otherwise, as may be appropriate to enforce or set aside the order of the division of the Adjustment Board: *Provided, however,* That such order may not be set aside except for failure of the division to comply with the requirements of this chapter, for failure of the order to conform, or confine itself, to matters within the scope of the division's jurisdiction, or for fraud or corruption by a member of the division making the order.

(q) If any employee or group of employees, or any carrier, is aggrieved by the failure of any division of the Adjustment Board to make an award in a dispute referred to it, or is aggrieved by any of the terms of an award or by the failure of the division to include certain terms in such award, then such employee or group of employees or carrier may file in any United States district court in which a petition under paragraph

(p) could be filed, a petition for review of the division's order. A copy of the petition shall be forthwith transmitted by the clerk of the court to the Adjustment Board. The Adjustment Board shall file in the court the record of the proceedings on which it based its action. The court shall have jurisdiction to affirm the order of the division, or to set it aside, in whole or in part, or it may remand the proceeding to the division for such further action as it may direct. On such review, the findings and order of the division shall be conclusive on the parties, except that the order of the division may be set aside, in whole or in part, or remanded to the division, for failure of the division to comply with the requirements of this chapter, for failure of the order to conform, or confine itself, to matters within the scope of the division's jurisdiction, or for fraud or corruption by a member of the division making the order. The judgment of the court shall be subject to review as provided in sections 1291 and 1254 of title 28, United States Code.

(r) All actions at law based upon the provisions of this section shall be begun within two years from the time the cause of action accrues under the award of the division of the Adjustment Board, and not after.

* * *

Second. Nothing in this section shall be construed to prevent any individual carrier, system, or group of carriers and any class or classes of its or their employees, all acting through their representatives, selected in accordance with the provisions of this Act, from mutually agreeing to the establishment of system, group, or regional boards of adjustment for the purpose of adjusting and deciding disputes of the character specified in this section. In the event that either party to such a system, group, or regional board of adjustment is dissatisfied with such arrangement, it may upon ninety days' notice to the other party elect to come under the jurisdiction of the Adjustment Board.

* * *

Sec. 4. First. * * * There is hereby established, as an independent agency in the executive branch of the Government, a board to be known as the "National Mediation Board," to be composed of three members appointed by the President, by and with the advice and consent of the Senate, not more than two of whom shall be of the same political party. Each member of the Mediation Board in office on January 1, 1965, shall be deemed to have been appointed for a term of office which shall expire on July 1 of the year his term would have otherwise expired. The terms of office of all successors shall expire three years after the expiration of the terms for which their predecessors were appointed; but any member appointed to fill a vacancy occurring prior to the expiration of the term of which his predecessor was appointed shall be appointed only for the unexpired term of his predecessor. * * *

A member of the Board may be removed by the President for inefficiency, neglect of duty, malfeasance in office, or ineligibility, but for no other cause.

* * *

Sec. 5. First. The parties, or either party, to a dispute between an employee or group of employees and a carrier may invoke the services of the Mediation Board in any of the following cases:

(a) A dispute concerning changes in rates of pay, rules, or working conditions not adjusted by the parties in conference.

(b) Any other dispute not referable to the National Railroad Adjustment Board and not adjusted in conference between the parties or where conferences are refused.

The Mediation Board may proffer its services in case any labor emergency is found by it to exist at any time.

In either event the said Board shall promptly put itself in communication with the parties to such controversy, and shall use its best efforts, by mediation, to bring them to agreement. If such efforts to bring about an amicable settlement through mediation shall be unsuccessful, the said Board shall at once endeavor as its final required action (except as provided in paragraph third of this section and in section 10 of this Act) to induce the parties to submit their controversy to arbitration, in accordance with the provisions of this Act.

If arbitration at the request of the Board shall be refused by one or both parties, the Board shall at once notify both parties in writing that its mediatory efforts have failed and for thirty days thereafter, unless in the intervening period the parties agree to arbitration, or an emergency board shall be created under section 10 of this Act, no change shall be made in the rates of pay, rules, or working conditions or establish practices in effect prior to the time the dispute arose.

* * *

Sec. 6. Carriers and representatives of the employees shall give at least thirty days' written notice of an intended change in agreements affecting rates of pay, rules, or working conditions, and the time and place for the beginning of conference between the representatives of the parties interested in such intended changes shall be agreed upon within ten days after the receipt of said notice, and said time shall be within the thirty days provided in the notice. In every case where such notice of intended change has been given, or conferences are being held with reference thereto, or the services of the Mediation Board have been requested by either party, or said Board has proffered its services, rates of pay, rules, or working conditions shall not be altered by the carrier until the controversy has been finally acted upon as required by section 5 of this Act, by the Mediation Board, unless a period of ten days has elapsed after termination of conferences without request for or proffer of the services of the Mediation Board.

Sec. 7. First. Whenever a controversy shall arise between a carrier or carriers and its or their employees which is not settled either in conference between representatives of the parties or by the appropriate adjustment board or through mediation, in the manner provided in the preceding sections, such controversy may, by agreement of the parties to such controversy, be submitted to the arbitration of a board of three (or, if the parties to the controversy so stipulate, of six) persons: *Provided, however*, That the failure or refusal of either party to submit a controversy to arbitration shall not be construed as a violation of any legal obligation imposed upon such party by the terms of this Act or otherwise.

Second. Such board of arbitration shall be chosen in the following manner:

(a) In the case of a board of three, the carrier or carriers and the representatives of the employees, parties respectively to the agreement to arbitrate, shall each name one arbitrator; the two arbitrators thus chosen shall select a third arbitrator. If the arbitrators chosen by the parties shall fail to name the third arbitrator within five days after their first meeting, such third arbitrator shall be named by the Mediation Board.

(b) In the case of a board of six, the carrier or carriers and the representatives of the employees, parties respectively to the agreement to arbitrate, shall each name two arbitrators; the four arbitrators thus chosen shall, by a majority vote, select the remaining two arbitrators. If the arbitrators chosen by the parties shall fail to name the two arbitrators within fifteen days after their first meeting, the said two arbitrators, or as many of them as have not been named, shall be named by the Mediation Board.

Third. (a) When the arbitrators selected by the respective parties have agreed upon the remaining arbitrator or arbitrators, they shall notify the Mediation Board, and, in the event of their failure to agree upon any or upon all of the necessary arbitrators within the period fixed by this Act, they shall, at the expiration of such period, notify the Mediation Board of the arbitrators selected, if any, or of their failure to make or complete such selection.

(b) The board of arbitration shall organize and select its own chairman and make all necessary rules for conducting its hearings: *Provided, however*, That the board of arbitration shall be bound to give the parties to the controversy a full and fair hearing, which shall include an opportunity to present evidence in support of their claims, and an opportunity to present their case in person, by counsel, or by other representative as they may respectively elect.

* * *

Sec. 9. First. The award of a board of arbitration, having been acknowledged as herein provided, shall be filed in the clerk's office of the district court designated in the agreement to arbitrate.

Second. An award acknowledged and filed as herein provided shall be conclusive on the parties as to the merits and facts of the controversy submitted to arbitration, and unless, within ten days after the filing of the award, a petition to impeach the award, on the grounds hereinafter set forth, shall be filed in the clerk's office of the court in which the award has been filed, the court shall enter judgment on the award, which judgment shall be final and conclusive on the parties.

Third. Such petition for the impeachment or contesting of any award so filed shall be entertained by the court only on one or more of the following grounds:

(a) That the award plainly does not conform to the substantive requirements laid down by this Act for such awards, or that the proceedings were not substantially in conformity with this Act;

(b) That the award does not conform, nor confine itself, to the stipulations of the agreement to arbitrate; or

(c) That a member of the board of arbitration rendering the award was guilty of fraud or corruption; or that a party to the arbitration practiced fraud or corruption which fraud or corruption affected the result of the arbitration. *Provided, however,* That no court shall entertain any such petition on the ground that an award is invalid for uncertainty; in such case the proper remedy shall be a submission of such award to a reconvened board, or subcommittee thereof, for interpretation, as provided by this Act: *Provided further,* That an award contested as herein provided shall be construed liberally by the court, with a view to favoring its validity, and that no award shall be set aside for trivial irregularity or clerical error, going only to form and not to substance.

* * *

Sec. 10. If a dispute between a carrier and its employees be not adjusted under the foregoing provisions of this Act and should, in the judgment of the Mediation Board, threaten substantially to interrupt interstate commerce to a degree such as to deprive any section of the country of essential transportation service, the Mediation Board shall notify the President, who may thereupon, in his discretion, create a board to investigate and report respecting such dispute. Such board shall be composed of such number of persons as to the President may seem desirable: *Provided, however,* That no member appointed shall be pecuniarily or otherwise interested in any organization of employees or any carrier. The compensation of the members of any such board shall be fixed by the President. Such board shall be created separately in each instance and it shall investigate promptly the facts as to the dispute and make a report thereon to the President within thirty days from the date of its creation.

* * *

After the creation of such board, and for thirty days after such board has made its report to the President, no change, except by agreement, shall be made by the parties to the controversy in the conditions out of which the dispute arose.

* * *

TITLE II

Sec. 201. All of the provisions of title I of this Act, except the provisions of section 3 thereof, are extended to and shall cover every common carrier by air engaged in interstate or foreign commerce, and every carrier by air transporting mail for or under contract with the United States Government, and every air pilot or other person who performs any work as an employee or subordinate official of such carrier or carriers, subject to its or their continuing authority to supervise and direct the manner of rendition of his service.

Sec. 202. The duties, requirements, penalties, benefits, and privileges prescribed and established by the provisions of title I of this Act, except section 3 thereof, shall apply to said carriers by air and their employees in the same manner and to the same extent as though such carriers and their employees were specifically included within the definition of "carrier" and "employee", respectively, in section 1 thereof.

Sec. 203. The parties or either party to a dispute between an employee or a group of employees and a carrier or carriers by air may invoke the services of the National Mediation Board and the jurisdiction of said Mediation Board is extended to any of the following cases:

(a) A dispute concerning changes in rates of pay, rules, or working conditions not adjusted by the parties in conference.

(b) Any other dispute not referable to an adjustment board, as hereinafter provided, and not adjusted in conference between the parties, or where conferences are refused.

The National Mediation Board may proffer its services in case any labor emergency is found by it to exist at any time.

The services of the Mediation Board may be invoked in a case under this title in the same manner and to the same extent as are the disputes covered by section 5 of title I of this Act.

Sec. 204. The disputes between an employee or group of employees and a carrier or carriers by air growing out of grievances, or out of interpretation or application of agreements concerning rates of pay, rules, or working conditions, including cases pending and unadjusted on the date of approval of this Act before the National Labor Relations Board, shall be handled in the usual manner up to and including the chief operating officer of the carrier designated to handle such disputes; but, failing to reach an adjustment in this manner, the disputes may be referred by petition of the parties or by either party to an appropriate adjustment board, as hereinafter provided, with a full statement of the facts and supporting data bearing upon the disputes.

It shall be the duty of every carrier and of its employees, acting through their representatives, selected in accordance with the provisions of this title, to establish a board of adjustment of jurisdiction not exceeding the jurisdiction which may be lawfully exercised by system, group, or regional boards of adjustment, under the authority of section 3, Title I, of this Act.

Such boards of adjustment may be established by agreement between employees and carriers either on any individual carrier, or system, or group of carriers by air and any class or classes of its or their employees; or pending the establishment of a permanent National Board of Adjustment as hereinafter provided. Nothing in this Act shall prevent said carriers by air, or any class or classes of their employees, both acting through their representatives selected in accordance with provisions of this title, from mutually agreeing to the establishment of a National Board of Adjustment of temporary duration and of similarly limited jurisdiction.

* * *

NATIONAL LABOR RELATIONS ACT*

49 Stat. 449 (1935), as amended; 29 U.S.C. §§ 151–69 (1988).

FINDINGS AND POLICIES

Sec. 1. The denial by **some** employers of the right of employees to organize and the refusal by **some** employers to accept the procedure of collective bargaining lead to strikes and other forms of industrial strife or unrest, which have the intent or the necessary effect of burdening or obstructing commerce by (a) impairing the efficiency, safety, or operation of the instrumentalities of commerce; (b) occurring in the current of commerce; (c) materially affecting, restraining, or controlling the flow of raw materials or manufactured or processed goods from or into the channels of commerce, or the prices of such materials or goods in commerce; or (d) causing diminution of employment and wages in such volume as substantially to impair or disrupt the market for goods flowing from or into the channels of commerce.

The inequality of bargaining power between employees who do not possess full freedom of association or actual liberty of contract, and employers who are organized in the corporate or other forms of ownership association substantially burdens and affects the flow of commerce, and tends to aggravate recurrent business depressions, by depressing wage rates and the purchasing power of wage earners in industry and by preventing the stabilization of competitive wage rates and working conditions within and between industries.

Experience has proved that protection by law of the right of employees to organize and bargain collectively safeguards commerce from injury, impairment, or interruption, and promotes the flow of commerce by removing certain recognized sources of industrial strife and unrest, by encouraging practices fundamental to the friendly adjustment of industrial disputes arising out of differences as to wages, hours, or other working conditions, and by restoring equality of bargaining power between employers and employees.

Experience has further demonstrated that certain practices by some labor organizations, their officers, and members have the intent or the necessary effect of burdening or obstructing commerce by preventing the free flow of goods in such commerce through strikes and other forms of industrial unrest or through concerted activities which impair the interest of the public in the free flow of such commerce. The elimination of such practices is

* The text of the original Wagner Act of 1935 is printed in roman type; the Taft-Hartley amendments of 1947 are in boldface type; the Landrum-Griffin amendments of 1959 are in italics; the 1974 amendments are underscored. Deleted matter is in brackets; bracketed matter in regular roman type was deleted in 1947, and bracketed matter in boldface type was deleted in 1959. Other amendments and deletions are specifically noted.

a necessary condition to the assurance of the rights herein guaranteed.

It is hereby declared to be the policy of the United States to eliminate the causes of certain substantial obstructions to the free flow of commerce and to mitigate and eliminate these obstructions when they have occurred by encouraging the practice and procedure of collective bargaining and by protecting the exercise by workers of full freedom of association, self-organization, and designation of representatives of their own choosing, for the purpose of negotiating the terms and conditions of their employment or other mutual aid or protection.

DEFINITIONS

Sec. 2. When used in this Act—

(1) The term "person" includes one or more individuals, labor organizations, partnerships, associations, corporations, legal representatives, trustees, trustees in bankruptcy, or receivers.

(2) The term "employer" includes any person acting [in the interest of] **as an agent** of an employer, directly or indirectly, but shall not include the United States **or any wholly owned Government corporation, or any Federal Reserve Bank,** or any State or political subdivision thereof, [**or any corporation or association operating a hospital, if no part of the net earnings inures to the benefit of any private shareholder or individual,**]* or any person subject to the Railway Labor Act, as amended from time to time, or any labor organization (other than when acting as an employer), or anyone acting in the capacity of officer or agent of such labor organization.

(3) The term "employee" shall include any employee, and shall not be limited to the employees of a particular employer, unless the Act explicitly states otherwise, and shall include any individual whose work has ceased as a consequence of, or in connection with, any current labor dispute or because of any unfair labor practice, and who has not obtained any other regular and substantially equivalent employment, but shall not include any individual employed as an agricultural laborer, or in the domestic service of any family or person at his home, or any individual employed by his parent or spouse, **or any individual having the status of an independent contractor, or any individual employed as a supervisor, or any individual employed by an employer subject to the Railway Labor Act, as amended from time to time, or by any other person who is not an employer as herein defined.**

(4) The term "representatives" includes any individual or labor organization.

(5) The term "labor organization" means any organization of any kind, or any agency or employee representation committee or plan, in which employees participate and which exists for the purpose, in whole

* The bracketed matter was deleted in 1974, by 88 Stat. 395 (1974).

or in part, of dealing with employers concerning grievances, labor disputes, wages, rates of pay, hours of employment, or conditions of work.

(6) The term "commerce" means trade, traffic, commerce, transportation, or communication among the several States, or between the District of Columbia or any Territory of the United States and any State or other Territory, or between any foreign country and any State, Territory, or the District of Columbia, or within the District of Columbia or any Territory, or between points in the same State but through any other State or any Territory or the District of Columbia or any foreign country.

(7) The term "affecting commerce" means in commerce, or burdening or obstructing commerce or the free flow of commerce, or having led or tending to lead to a labor dispute burdening or obstructing commerce or the free flow of commerce.

(8) The term "unfair labor practice" means any unfair labor practice listed in section 8.

(9) The term "labor dispute" includes any controversy concerning terms, tenure or conditions of employment, or concerning the association or representation of persons in negotiating, fixing, maintaining, changing, or seeking to arrange terms or conditions of employment, regardless of whether the disputants stand in the proximate relation of employer and employee.

(10) The term "National Labor Relations Board" means the National Labor Relations Board provided for in section 3 of this Act.

(11) The term "supervisor" means any individual having authority, in the interest of the employer, to hire, transfer, suspend, lay off, recall, promote, discharge, assign, reward, or discipline other employees, or responsibly to direct them, or to adjust their grievances, or effectively to recommend such action, if in connection with the foregoing the exercise of such authority is not of a merely routine or clerical nature, but requires the use of independent judgment.

(12) The term "professional employee" means—

(a) any employee engaged in work (i) predominantly intellectual and varied in character as opposed to routine mental, manual, mechanical, or physical work; (ii) involving the consistent exercise of discretion and judgment in its performance; (iii) of such a character that the output produced or the result accomplished cannot be standardized in relation to a given period of time; (iv) requiring knowledge of an advanced type in a field of science or learning customarily acquired by a prolonged course of specialized intellectual instruction and study in an institution of higher learning or a hospital, as distinguished from a general academic education or from an apprenticeship or from

training in the performance of routine mental, manual, or physical processes; or

(b) any employee, who (i) has completed the courses of specialized intellectual instruction and study described in clause (iv) of paragraph (a), and (ii) is performing related work under the supervision of a professional person to qualify himself to become a professional employee as defined in paragraph (a).

(13) In determining whether any person is acting as an "agent" of another person so as to make such other person responsible for his acts, the question of whether the specific acts performed were actually authorized or subsequently ratified shall not be controlling.

(14) The term "health care institution" shall include any hospital, convalescent hospital, health maintenance organization, health clinic, nursing home, extended care facility, or other institution devoted to the care of sick, infirm, or aged person.

NATIONAL LABOR RELATIONS BOARD

Sec. 3.* (a) The National Labor Relations Board (hereinafter called the "Board") created by this Act prior to its amendment by the Labor Management Relations Act, 1947, is continued as an agency of the United States, except that the Board shall consist of five instead of three members, appointed by the President by and with the advice and consent of the Senate. Of the two additional members so provided for, one shall be appointed for a term of five years and the other for a term of two years. Their successors, and the successors of the other members, shall be appointed for terms of five years each, excepting that any individual chosen to fill a vacancy shall be appointed only for the unexpired term of the member whom he shall succeed. The President shall designate one member to serve as Chairman of the Board. Any member of the Board may be removed by the President, upon notice and hearing, for neglect of duty or malfeasance in office, but for no other cause.

(b) **The Board is authorized to delegate to any group of three or more members any or all of the powers which it may itself exercise.** *The Board is also authorized to delegate to its regional directors its powers under section 9 to determine the unit appropriate for the purpose of collective bargaining, to investigate and provide for hearings, and determine whether a question of representation exists, and to direct an election or take a secret ballot under subsection (c) or (e) of section 9 and certify the results thereof, except that upon the filing of a request*

* The changes made in Sections 3 and 4 by the Taft-Hartley amendments were so extensive, that the typeface designations for these two sections show only the 1947 and 1959 amendments.

therefor with the Board by any interested person, the Board may review any action of a regional director delegated to him under this paragraph, but such a review shall not, unless specifically ordered by the Board, operate as a stay of any action taken by the regional director. **A vacancy in the Board shall not impair the right of the remaining members to exercise all of the powers of the Board, and three members of the Board shall, at all times, constitute a quorum of the Board, except that two members shall constitute a quorum of any group designated pursuant to the first sentence hereof. The Board shall have an official seal which shall be judicially noticed.**

(c) The Board shall at the close of each fiscal year make a report in writing to Congress and to the President [stating in detail the cases it has heard, the decisions it has rendered, the names, salaries, and duties of all employees and officers in the employ or under the supervision of the Board, and an account of all moneys it has disbursed.]* summarizing significant case activities and operations for that fiscal year.

(d) **There shall be a General Counsel of the Board who shall be appointed by the President, by and with the advice and consent of the Senate, for a term of four years. The General Counsel of the Board shall exercise general supervision over all attorneys employed by the Board (other than administrative law judges** and legal assistants to Board members) and over the officers and employees in the regional offices. He shall have final authority, on behalf of the Board, in respect of the investigation of charges and issuance of complaints under section 10, and in respect of the prosecution of such complaints before the Board, and shall have such other duties as the Board may prescribe or as may be provided by law.** *In case of a vacancy in the office of the General Counsel the President is authorized to designate the officer or employee who shall act as General Counsel during such vacancy, but no person or persons so designated shall so act (1) for more than forty days when the Congress is in session unless a nomination to fill such vacancy shall have been submitted to the Senate, or (2) after the adjournment sine die of the session of the Senate in which such nomination was submitted.*

Sec. 4. (a) Each member of the Board and the General Counsel of the Board [shall receive a salary of $12,000 per annum,] shall be eligible for reappointment, and shall not engage in any other business, vocation, or employment. The Board shall appoint an executive secretary, and such attorneys, examiners, and regional directors, and such other employees as it may from time to time find necessary for the proper performance of its duties. The Board may not employ any attorneys for the purpose of reviewing transcripts of hearings or preparing drafts of

* The bracketed matter was deleted in part in 1975 and in part in 1982, and the matter following was added in 1982.

** The title "administrative law judge" was adopted in 5 U.S.C. § 3105, in 1972.

opinions except that any attorney employed for assignment as a legal assistant to any Board member may for such Board member review such transcripts and prepare such drafts. No administrative law judge's report shall be reviewed, either before or after its publication, by any person other than a member of the Board or his legal assistant, and no administrative law judge shall advise or consult with the Board with respect to exceptions taken to his findings, rulings, or recommendations. The Board may establish or utilize such regional, local, or other agencies, and utilize such voluntary and uncompensated services, as may from time to time be needed. Attorneys appointed under this section may, at the direction of the Board, appear for and represent the Board in any case in court. Nothing in this Act shall be construed to authorize the Board to appoint individuals for the purpose of conciliation or mediation, or for economic analysis.

(b) All of the expenses of the Board, including all necessary traveling and subsistence expenses outside the District of Columbia incurred by the members or employees of the Board under its orders, shall be allowed and paid on the presentation of itemized vouchers therefor approved by the Board or by any individual it designates for that purpose.

Sec. 5. The principal office of the Board shall be in the District of Columbia, but it may meet and exercise any or all of its powers at any other place. The Board may, by one or more of its members or by such agents or agencies as it may designate, prosecute any inquiry necessary to its functions in any part of the United States. A member who participates in such an inquiry shall not be disqualified from subsequently participating in a decision of the Board in the same case.

Sec. 6. The Board shall have authority from time to time to make, amend, and rescind, **in the manner prescribed by the Administrative Procedure Act,** such rules and regulations as may be necessary to carry out the provisions of this Act. [Such rules and regulations shall be effective upon publication in the manner which the Board shall prescribe.]

RIGHTS OF EMPLOYEES

Sec. 7. Employees shall have the right to self-organization, to form, join, or assist labor organizations, to bargain collectively through representatives of their own choosing, and to engage in other concerted activities for the purpose of collective bargaining or other mutual aid or protection, **and shall also have the right to refrain from any or all of such activities except to the extent that such right may be affected by an agreement requiring membership in a labor organization as a condition of employment as authorized in section 8(a)(3).**

UNFAIR LABOR PRACTICES

Sec. 8. (a) It shall be an unfair labor practice for an employer—

(1) to interfere with, restrain, or coerce employees in the exercise of the rights guaranteed in section 7;

(2) to dominate or interfere with the formation or administration of any labor organization or contribute financial or other support to it: *Provided*, That subject to rules and regulations made and published by the Board pursuant to section 6, an employer shall not be prohibited from permitting employees to confer with him during working hours without loss of time or pay;

(3) by discrimination in regard to hire or tenure of employment or any term or condition of employment to encourage or discourage membership in any labor organization: *Provided*, That nothing in this Act, or in any other statute of the United States, shall preclude an employer from making an agreement with a labor organization (not established, maintained, or assisted by any action defined in **section 8(a) of** this Act as an unfair labor practice) to require as a condition of employment membership therein **on or after the thirtieth day following the beginning of such employment or the effective date of such agreement, whichever is the later, (i)** if such labor organization is the representative of the employees as provided in section 9(a), in the appropriate collective-bargaining unit covered by such agreement when made, **[and has at the time the agreement was made or within the preceding twelve months received from the Board a notice of compliance with Section 9(f), (g), (h)], and (ii) unless following an election held as provided in section 9(e) within one year preceding the effective date of such agreement, the Board shall have certified that at least a majority of the employees eligible to vote in such election have voted to rescind the authority of such labor organization to make such an agreement:*** ***Provided further*, That no employer shall justify any discrimination against an employee for nonmembership in a labor organization (A) if he has reasonable grounds for believing that such membership was not available to the employee on the same terms and conditions generally applicable to other members, or (B) if he has reasonable grounds for believing that membership was denied or terminated for reasons other than the failure of the employee to tender the periodic dues and the initiation fees uniformly required as a condition of acquiring or retaining membership;**

(4) to discharge or otherwise discriminate against an employee because he has filed charges or given testimony under this Act;

* The (ii) provision was added in 1951 by 65 Stat. 601.

(5) to refuse to bargain collectively with the representatives of his employees, subject to the provisions of section 9(a).

(b) **It shall be an unfair labor practice for a labor organization or its agents—**

(1) to restrain or coerce (A) employees in the exercise of the rights guaranteed in section 7: *Provided*, That this paragraph shall not impair the right of a labor organization to prescribe its own rules with respect to the acquisition or retention of membership therein; or (B) an employer in the selection of his representatives for the purposes of collective bargaining or the adjustment of grievances;

(2) to cause or attempt to cause an employer to discriminate against an employee in violation of subsection (a)(3) or to discriminate against an employee with respect to whom membership in such organization has been denied or terminated on some ground other than his failure to tender the periodic dues and the initiation fees uniformly required as a condition of acquiring or retaining membership;

(3) to refuse to bargain collectively with an employer, provided it is the representative of his employees subject to the provisions of section 9(a);

(4)*(i)* **to engage in, or to induce or encourage [the employees of any employer]** *any individual employed by any person engaged in commerce or in an industry affecting commerce* **to engage in, a strike or a [concerted] refusal in the course of [their]** *his* **employment to use, manufacture, process, transport, or otherwise handle or work on any goods, articles, materials, or commodities or to perform any services[,];** *or (ii) to threaten, coerce, or restrain any person engaged in commerce or in an industry affecting commerce,* **where** *in either case* **an object thereof is—**

(A) forcing or requiring any employer or self-employed person to join any labor or employer organization [or any employer or other person to cease using, selling, handling, transporting, or otherwise dealing in the products of any other producer, processor, or manufacturer, or to cease doing business with any other person;] *or to enter into any agreement which is prohibited by section 8(e);*

(B) forcing or requiring any **[any employer or other]** *person to cease using, selling, handling, transporting, or otherwise dealing in the products of any other producer, processor, or manufacturer, or to cease doing business with any other person, or* **forcing or requiring any other employer to recognize or bargain with a labor organization as the**

representative of his employees unless such labor organization has been certified as the representative of such employees under the provisions of section 9[;]; *Provided, That nothing contained in this clause (B) shall be construed to make unlawful, where not otherwise unlawful, any primary strike or primary picketing;*

(C) forcing or requiring any employer to recognize or bargain with a particular labor organization as the representative of his employees if another labor organization has been certified as the representative of such employees under the provisions of section 9;

(D) forcing or requiring any employer to assign particular work to employees in a particular labor organization or in a particular trade, craft, or class rather than to employees in another labor organization or in another trade, craft, or class, unless such employer is failing to conform to an order or certification of the Board determining the bargaining representative for employees performing such work:

***Provided*, That nothing contained in this subsection (b) shall be construed to make unlawful a refusal by any person to enter upon the premises of any employer (other than his own employer), if the employees of such employer are engaged in a strike ratified or approved by a representative of such employees whom such employer is required to recognize under this Act:** *Provided further, That for the purposes of this paragraph (4) only, nothing contained in such paragraph shall be construed to prohibit publicity, other than picketing, for the purpose of truthfully advising the public, including consumers and members of a labor organization, that a product or products are produced by an employer with whom the labor organization has a primary dispute and are distributed by another employer, as long as such publicity does not have an effect of inducing any individual employed by any person other than the primary employer in the course of his employment to refuse to pick up, deliver, or transport any goods, or not to perform any services, at the establishment of the employer engaged in such distribution:*

(5) to require of employees covered by an agreement authorized under subsection (a)(3) the payment, as a condition precedent to becoming a member of such organization, of a fee in an amount which the Board finds excessive or discriminatory under all the circumstances. In making such a finding, the Board shall consider, among other relevant factors, the practices and customs of labor organizations in the particular industry, and the wages currently paid to the employees affected; [and]

(6) to cause or attempt to cause an employer to pay or deliver or agree to pay or deliver any money or other thing of value, in the nature of an exaction, for services which are not performed or not to be performed[.]; *and*

(7) to picket or cause to be picketed, or threaten to picket or cause to be picketed, any employer where an object thereof is forcing or requiring an employer to recognize or bargain with a labor organization as the representatives of his employees, or forcing or requiring the employees of an employer to accept or select such labor organization as their collective bargaining representative, unless such labor organization is currently certified as the representative of such employees:

(A) where the employer has lawfully recognized in accordance with this Act any other labor organization and a question concerning representation may not appropriately be raised under section 9(c) of this Act.

(B) where within the preceding twelve months a valid election under section 9(c) of this Act has been conducted, or

(C) where such picketing has been conducted without a petition under section 9(c) being filed within a reasonable period of time not to exceed thirty days from the commencement of such picketing: Provided, That when such a petition has been filed the Board shall forthwith, without regard to the provisions of section 9(c)(1) or the absence of a showing of a substantial interest on the part of the labor organization, direct an election in such unit as the Board finds to be appropriate and shall certify the results thereof: Provided further, That nothing in this subparagraph (C) shall be construed to prohibit any picketing or other publicity for the purpose of truthfully advising the public (including consumers) that an employer does not employ members of, or have a contract with, a labor organization, unless an effect of such picketing is to induce any individual employed by any other person in the course of his employment, not to pick up, deliver or transport any goods or not to perform any services.

Nothing in this paragraph (7) shall be construed to permit any act which would otherwise be an unfair labor practice under this section 8(b).

(c) The expressing of any views, argument, or opinion, or the dissemination thereof, whether in written, printed, graphic, or visual form, shall not constitute or be evidence of an unfair labor practice under any of the provisions of this Act, if such expression contains no threat of reprisal or force or promise of benefit.

(d) For the purposes of this section, to bargain collectively is the performance of the mutual obligation of the employer and

the representative of the employees to meet at reasonable times and confer in good faith with respect to wages, hours, and other terms and conditions of employment, or the negotiation of an agreement, or any question arising thereunder, and the execution of a written contract incorporating any agreement reached if requested by either party, but such obligation does not compel either party to agree to a proposal or require the making of a concession: *Provided*, That where there is in effect a collective-bargaining contract covering employees in an industry affecting commerce, the duty to bargain collectively shall also mean that no party to such contract shall terminate or modify such contract, unless the party desiring such termination or modification—

(1) serves a written notice upon the other party to the contract of the proposed termination or modification sixty days prior to the expiration date thereof, or in the event such contract contains no expiration date, sixty days prior to the time it is proposed to make such termination or modification;

(2) offers to meet and confer with the other party for the purpose of negotiating a new contract or a contract containing the proposed modifications;

(3) notifies the Federal Mediation and Conciliation Service within thirty days after such notice of the existence of a dispute, and simultaneously therewith notifies any State or Territorial agency established to mediate and conciliate disputes within the State or Territory where the dispute occurred, provided no agreement has been reached by that time; and

(4) continues in full force and effect, without resorting to strike or lock-out, all the terms and conditions of the existing contract for a period of sixty days after such notice is given or until the expiration date of such contract, whichever occurs later:

The duties imposed upon employers, employees, and labor organizations by paragraphs (2), (3), and (4) shall become inapplicable upon an intervening certification of the Board, under which the labor organization or individual, which is a party to the contract, has been superseded as or ceased to be the representative of the employees subject to the provisions of section 9(a), and the duties so imposed shall not be construed as requiring either party to discuss or agree to any modification of the terms and conditions contained in a contract for a fixed period, if such modification is to become effective before such terms and conditions can be reopened under the provisions of the contract. Any employee who engages in a strike within [the sixty-day] <u>any notice</u> period specified in this subsection, <u>or who</u>

engages in any strike within the appropriate period specified in subsection (g) of this section, **shall lose his status as an employee of the employer engaged in the particular labor dispute, for the purposes of sections 8, 9, and 10 of this Act, but such loss of status for such employee shall terminate if and when he is reemployed by such employer.** Whenever the collective bargaining involves employees of a health care institution, the provisions of this section 8(d) shall be modified as follows:

(A) The notice of section 8(d)(1) shall be ninety days; the notice of section 8(d)(3) shall be sixty days; and the contract period of section 8(d)(4) shall be ninety days.

(B) Where the bargaining is for an initial agreement following certification or recognition, at least thirty days' notice of the existence of a dispute shall be given by the labor organization to the agencies set forth in section 8(d)(3).

(C) After notice is given to the Federal Mediation and Conciliation Service under either clause (A) or (B) of this sentence, the Service shall promptly communicate with the parties and use its best efforts, by mediation and conciliation, to bring them to agreement. The parties shall participate fully and promptly in such meetings as may be undertaken by the Service for the purpose of aiding in a settlement of the dispute.

(e) It shall be an unfair labor practice for any labor organization and any employer to enter into any contract or agreement, express or implied, whereby such employer ceases or refrains or agrees to cease or refrain from handling, using, selling, transporting or otherwise dealing in any of the products of any other employer, or to cease doing business with any other person, and any contract or agreement entered into heretofore or hereafter containing such an agreement shall be to such extent unenforceable and void: Provided, That nothing in this subsection (e) shall apply to an agreement between a labor organization and an employer in the construction industry relating to the contracting or subcontracting of work to be done at the site of the construction, alteration, painting, or repair of a building, structure, or other work: Provided further, That for the purposes of this subsection (e) and section 8(b)(4)(B) the terms "any employer", "any person engaged in commerce or an industry affecting commerce", and "any person" when used in relation to the terms "any other producer, processor, or manufacturer", "any other employer", or "any other person" shall not include persons in the relation of a jobber, manufacturer, contractor, or subcontractor working on the goods or premises of the jobber or manufacturer or performing parts of an integrated process of production in the apparel and clothing industry: Provided further, That nothing in this Act shall prohibit the enforcement of any agreement which is within the foregoing exception.

(f) It shall not be an unfair labor practice under subsections (a) and (b) of this section for an employer engaged primarily in the building and construction industry to make an agreement covering employees engaged (or who, upon their employment, will be engaged) in the building and construction industry with a labor organization of which building and construction employees are members (not established, maintained, or assisted by any action defined in section 8(a) of this Act as an unfair practice) because (1) the majority status of such labor organization has not been established under the provisions of section 9 of this Act lab prior to the making of such agreement, or (2) such agreement requires as a condition of employment, membership in such labor organization after the seventh day following the beginning of such employment or the effective date of the agreement, whichever is later, or (3) such agreement requires the employer to notify such labor organization of opportunities for employment with such employer, or gives such labor organization an opportunity to refer qualified applicants for such employment, or (4) such agreement specifies minimum training or experience qualifications for employment or provides for priority in opportunities for employment based upon length of service with such employer, in the industry or in the particular geographical area: Provided, That nothing in this subsection shall set aside the final proviso to section 8(a)(3) of this Act: Provided further, That any agreement which would be invalid, but for clause (1) of this subsection, shall not be a bar to a petition filed pursuant to section 9(c) or 9(e).*

(g) A labor organization before engaging in any strike, picketing, or other concerted refusal to work at any health care institution shall, not less than ten days prior to such action, notify the institution in writing and the Federal Mediation and Conciliation Service of that intention, except that in the case of bargaining for an initial agreement following certification or recognition the notice required by this subsection shall not be given until the expiration of the period specified in clause (B) of the last sentence of section 8(d) of this Act. The notice shall state the date and time that such action will commence. The notice, once given, may be extended by the written agreement of both parties.

REPRESENTATIVES AND ELECTIONS

Sec. 9. (a) Representatives designated or selected for the purposes of collective bargaining by the majority of the employees in a unit appropriate for such purposes, shall be the exclusive representatives of all the employees in such unit for the purposes of collective bargaining in respect to rates of pay, wages, hours of employment, or other conditions of employment: *Provided*, That any individual employee or a

* Sec. 8(f) was inserted in the Act by subsec. (a) of Sec. 705 of Public Law 86–257. Sec. 705(b) provides:

Nothing contained in the amendment made by subsection (a) shall be construed as authorizing the execution or application of agreements requiring membership in a labor organization as a condition of employment in any State or Territory in which such execution or application is prohibited by State or Territorial law.

group of employees shall have the right at any time to present grievances to their employer **and to have such grievances adjusted, without the intervention of the bargaining representative, as long as the adjustment is not inconsistent with the terms of a collective-bargaining contract or agreement then in effect: *Provided further*, That the bargaining representative has been given opportunity to be present at such adjustment.**

(b) The Board shall decide in each case whether, in order to assure to employees the fullest freedom in exercising the rights guaranteed by this Act, the unit appropriate for the purposes of collective bargaining shall be the employer unit, craft unit, plant unit, or subdivision thereof: ***Provided*, That the Board shall not (1) decide that any unit is appropriate for such purposes if such unit includes both professional employees and employees who are not professional employees unless a majority of such professional employees vote for inclusion in such unit; or (2) decide that any craft unit is inappropriate for such purposes on the ground that a different unit has been established by a prior Board determination, unless a majority of the employees in the proposed craft unit vote against separate representation or (3) decide that any unit is appropriate for such purposes if it includes, together with other employees, any individual employed as a guard to enforce against employees and other persons rules to protect property of the employer or to protect the safety of persons on the employer's premises; but no labor organization shall be certified as the representative of employees in a bargaining unit of guards if such organization admits to membership, or is affiliated directly or indirectly with an organization which admits to membership, employees other than guards.**

[(c) Whenever a question affecting commerce arises concerning the representation of employees, the Board may investigate such controversy and certify to the parties, in writing, the name or names of the representatives that have been designated or selected. In any such investigation, the Board shall provide for an appropriate hearing upon due notice, either in conjunction with a proceeding under section 10 or otherwise, and may take a secret ballot of employees, or utilize any other suitable method to ascertain such representatives.]

(c)(1) Whenever a petition shall have been filed, in accordance with such regulations as may be prescribed by the Board—

(A) by an employee or group of employees or any individual or labor organization acting in their behalf alleging that a substantial number of employees (i) wish to be represented for collective bargaining and that their employer declines to recognize their representative as the representative defined in section 9(a), or (ii) assert that the

individual or labor organization, which has been certified or is being currently recognized by their employer as the bargaining representative, is no longer a representative as defined in section 9(a); or

(B) by an employer, alleging that one or more individuals or labor organizations have presented to him a claim to be recognized as the representative defined in section 9(a);

the Board shall investigate such petition and if it has reasonable cause to believe that a question of representation affecting commerce exists shall provide for an appropriate hearing upon due notice. Such hearing may be conducted by an officer or employee of the regional office, who shall not make any recommendations with respect thereto. If the Board finds upon the record of such hearing that such a question of representation exists, it shall direct an election by secret ballot and shall certify the results thereof.

(2) In determining whether or not a question of representation affecting commerce exists, the same regulations and rules of decision shall apply irrespective of the identity of the persons filing the petition or the kind of relief sought and in no case shall the Board deny a labor organization a place on the ballot by reason of an order with respect to such labor organization or its predecessor not issued in conformity with section 10(c).

(3) No election shall be directed in any bargaining unit or any subdivision within which, in the preceding twelve-month period, a valid election shall have been held. Employees [on strike] *engaged in an economic strike* **who are not entitled to reinstatement shall [not] be eligible to vote** *under such regulations as the Board shall find are consistent with the purposes and provisions of this Act in any election conducted within twelve months after the commencement of the strike.* **In any election where none of the choices on the ballot receives a majority, a run-off shall be conducted, the ballot providing for a selection between the two choices receiving the largest and second largest number of valid votes cast in the election.**

(4) Nothing in this section shall be construed to prohibit the waiving of hearings by stipulation for the purpose of a consent election in conformity with regulations and rules of decision of the Board.

(5) In determining whether a unit is appropriate for the purposes specified in subsection (b) the extent to which the employees have organized shall not be controlling.

(d) Whenever an order of the Board made pursuant to section 10(c) is based in whole or in part upon facts certified following an investigation pursuant to subsection (c) of this section and there is a petition for the enforcement or review of such order, such certification and the record of such investigation shall be included in the transcript of the entire record required to be filed under section 10(e) or 10(f), and thereupon the decree of the court enforcing, modifying, or setting aside in whole or in part the order of the Board shall be made and entered upon the pleadings, testimony, and proceedings set forth in such transcript.

(e)*(1) Upon the filing with the Board, by 30 per centum or more of the employees in a bargaining unit covered by an agreement between their employer and a labor organization made pursuant to section 8(a)(3), of a petition alleging they desire that such authority be rescinded, the Board shall take a secret ballot of the employees in such unit, and shall certify the results thereof to such labor organization and to the employer.

(2) No election shall be conducted pursuant to this subsection in any bargaining unit or any subdivision within which, in the preceding twelve-month period, a valid election shall have been held.

[Subsections (f), (g) and (h) were deleted by the Labor-Management Reporting and Disclosure Act.]

PREVENTION OF UNFAIR LABOR PRACTICES

Sec. 10. (a) The Board is empowered, as hereinafter provided, to prevent any person from engaging in any unfair labor practice (listed in section 8) affecting commerce. This power shall not be affected by any other means of adjustment or prevention that has been or may be established by agreement, law, or otherwise: ***Provided*, That the Board is empowered by agreement with any agency of any State or Territory to cede to such agency jurisdiction over any cases in any industry (other than mining, manufacturing, communications, and transportation except where predominantly local in character) even though such cases may involve labor disputes affecting commerce, unless the provision of the State of Territorial statute applicable to the determination of such cases by such agency is inconsistent with the corresponding provision of this Act or has received a construction inconsistent therewith.**

(b) Whenever it is charged that any person has engaged in or is engaging in any such unfair labor practice, the Board, or any agent or agency designated by the Board for such purposes, shall have power to

* As enacted in 1947, Section 9(e) had three subsections. In 1951, the first subsection was deleted and the two remaining subsections were renumbered (1) and (2). 65 Stat. 601. The deleted subsection required, as a condition to the inclusion of a union-shop provision in a collective agreement, that a majority of employees authorize such inclusion in a Board-conducted election.

issue and cause to be served upon such person a complaint stating the charges in that respect, and containing a notice of hearing before the Board or a member thereof, or before a designated agent or agency, at a place therein fixed, not less than five days after the serving of said complaint: ***Provided*,** **That no complaint shall issue based upon any unfair labor practice occurring more than six months prior to the filing of the charge with the Board and the service of a copy thereof upon the person against whom such charge is made, unless the person aggrieved thereby was prevented from filing such charge by reason of service in the armed forces, in which event the six-month period shall be computed from the day of his discharge.** Any such complaint may be amended by the member, agent, or agency conducting the hearing or the Board in its discretion at any time prior to the issuance of an order based thereon. The person so complained of shall have the right to file an answer to the original or amended complaint and to appear in person or otherwise and give testimony at the place and time fixed in the complaint. In the discretion of the member, agent, or agency conducting the hearing or the Board, any other person may be allowed to intervene in the said proceeding and to present testimony. [In any such proceeding the rules of evidence prevailing in courts of law or equity shall not be controlling.] **Any such proceeding shall, so far as practicable, be conducted in accordance with the rules of evidence applicable in the district courts of the United States under the rules of civil procedure for the district courts of the United States, adopted by the Supreme Court of the United States pursuant to section 2072 of Title 28.**

(c) The testimony taken by such member, agent, or agency or the Board shall be reduced to writing and filed with the Board. Thereafter, in its discretion, the Board upon notice may take further testimony or hear argument. If upon [all] **the preponderance of** the testimony taken the Board shall be of the opinion that any person named in the complaint has engaged in or is engaging in any such unfair labor practice, then the Board shall state its findings of fact and shall issue and cause to be served on such person an order requiring such person to cease and desist from such unfair labor practice, and to take such affirmative action including reinstatement of employees with or without back pay, as will effectuate the policies of this Act: ***Provided*, That where an order directs reinstatement of an employee, back pay may be required of the employer or labor organization, as the case may be, responsible for the discrimination suffered by him: *And provided further*, That in determining whether a complaint shall issue alleging a violation of section 8(a)(1) or section 8(a)(2), and in deciding such cases, the same regulations and rules of decision shall apply irrespective of whether or not the labor organization affected is affiliated with a labor organization national or international in scope.** Such order may further require such person to make reports from time to time showing the extent to which it has complied with the order.

If upon [all] **the preponderance of** the testimony taken the Board shall not be of the opinion that the person named in the complaint has engaged in or is engaging in any such unfair labor practice, then the Board shall state its findings of fact and shall issue an order dismissing the said complaint. **No order of the Board shall require the reinstatement of any individual as an employee who has been suspended or discharged, or the payment to him of any back pay, if such individual was suspended or discharged for cause. In case the evidence is presented before a member of the Board, or before an administrative law judge or judges* thereof, such member, or such judge or judges, as the case may be, shall issue and cause to be served on the parties to the proceeding a proposed report, together with a recommended order, which shall be filed with the Board, and if no exceptions are filed within twenty days after service thereof upon such parties, or within such further period as the Board may authorize, such recommended order shall become the order of the Board and become effective as therein prescribed.**

(d) Until [**a transcript of**] the record in a case shall have been filed in a court, as hereinafter provided, the Board may at any time, upon reasonable notice and in such manner as it shall deem proper, modify or set aside, in whole or in part, any finding or order made or issued by it.

(e) The Board shall have power to petition any [United States] court of appeals of the United States [(including the United States court of appeals for the District of Columbia)] or if all the courts of appeals to which application may be made are in vacation, any [United States] district court *of the United States*, within any circuit or district, respectively, wherein the unfair labor practice in question occurred or wherein such person resides or transacts business, for the enforcement of such order and for appropriate temporary relief or restraining order, and shall [certify and] file in the court [a transcript of] the [entire] record in the proceedings, [including the pleadings and testimony upon which such order was entered and the findings and order of the Board.] *as printed in section 2112 of Title 28.* Upon [such filing] *the filing of such petition*, the court shall cause notice thereof to be served upon such person, and thereupon shall have jurisdiction of the proceeding and of the question determined therein, and shall have power to grant such temporary relief or restraining order as it deems just and proper, and to make and enter [upon the pleadings, testimony, and proceedings set forth in such transcript] a decree enforcing, modifying, and enforcing as so modified, or setting aside in whole or in part the order of the Board. No objection that has not been urged before the Board, its member, agent, or agency, shall be considered by the court, unless the failure or neglect to urge such objection shall be excused because of extraordinary circumstances. The findings of the Board with respect to questions of fact

---

* The title "administrative law judge" was adopted in 5 U.S.C. § 3105, in 1972.

if supported by **substantial** evidence **on the record considered as a whole** shall be conclusive. If either party shall apply to the court for leave to adduce additional evidence and shall show to the satisfaction of the court that such additional evidence is material and that there were reasonable grounds for the failure to adduce such evidence in the hearing before the Board, its member, agent, or agency, the court may order such additional evidence to be taken before the Board, its member, agent, or agency, and to be made a part of [the transcript] *record*. The Board may modify its findings as to the facts, or make new findings, by reason of additional evidence so taken and filed, and it shall file such modified or new findings, which findings with respect to questions of fact if supported by **substantial** evidence **on the record considered as a whole** shall be conclusive, and shall file its recommendations, if any, for the modification or setting aside of its original order. *Upon the filing of the record with it* the jurisdiction of the court shall be exclusive and its judgment and decree shall be final, except that the same shall be subject to review by the appropriate circuit court of appeals if application was made to the district court as hereinabove provided, and by the Supreme Court of the United States upon writ of certiorari or certification as provided in section 1254 of Title 28.

(f) Any person aggrieved by a final order of the Board granting or denying in whole or in part the relief sought may obtain a review of such order in any United States court of appeals in the circuit wherein the unfair labor practice in question was alleged to have been engaged in or wherein such person resides or transacts business, or in the United States Court of Appeals for the District of Columbia, by filing in such court a written petition praying that the order of the Board be modified or set aside. A copy of such petition shall be forthwith [served upon the Board] *transmitted by the clerk of the court to the Board* and thereupon the aggrieved party shall file in the court [a transcript of] the [entire] record in the proceeding, certified by the Board, [including the pleading and testimony upon which the order complained of was entered, and the findings and order of the Board.] *as provided in section 2112 of Title 28*. Upon [such filing,] *the filing of such petition*, the court shall proceed in the same manner as in the case of an application by the Board under subsection (e) *of this section*, and shall have the same exclusive jurisdiction to grant to the Board such temporary relief or restraining order as it deems just and proper, and in like manner to make and enter a decree enforcing, modifying, and enforcing as so modified, or setting aside in whole or in part the order of the Board; the findings of the Board with respect to questions of fact if supported by **substantial** evidence **on the record considered as a whole** shall in like manner be conclusive.

(g) The commencement of proceedings under subsection (e) or (f) of this section shall not, unless specifically ordered by the court, operate as a stay of the Board's order.

(h) When granting appropriate temporary relief or a restraining order, or making and entering a decree enforcing, modifying, and enforcing as so modified, or setting aside in whole or in part an order of the Board, as provided in this section, the jurisdiction of courts sitting in equity shall not be limited by sections 101 to 115 of title 29, United States Code.*

(i) [Repealed.]

(j) The Board shall have power, upon issuance of a complaint as provided in subsection (b) charging that any person has engaged in or is engaging in an unfair labor practice, to petition any United States district court within any district wherein the unfair labor practice in question is alleged to have occurred or wherein such person resides or transacts business, for appropriate temporary relief or restraining order. Upon the filing of any such petition the court shall cause notice thereof to be served upon such person, and thereupon shall have jurisdiction to grant to the Board such temporary relief or restraining order as it deems just and proper.

(k) Whenever it is charged that any person has engaged in an unfair labor practice within the meaning of paragraph (4)(D) of section 8(b), the Board is empowered and directed to hear and determine the dispute out of which such unfair labor practice shall have arisen, unless, within ten days after notice that such charge has been filed, the parties to such dispute submit to the Board satisfactory evidence that they have adjusted, or agreed upon methods for the voluntary adjustment of, the dispute. Upon compliance by the parties to the dispute with the decision of the Board or upon such voluntary adjustment of the dispute, such charge shall be dismissed.

(*l*) Whenever it is charged that any person has engaged in an unfair labor practice within the meaning of paragraph (4)(A), (B), or (C) of section 8(b), *or section 8(e) or section 8(b)(7)* **the preliminary investigation of such charge shall be made forthwith and given priority over all other cases except cases of like character in the office where it is filed or to which it is referred. If, after such investigation, the officer or regional attorney to whom the matter may be referred has reasonable cause to believe such charge is true and that a complaint should issue, he shall, on behalf of the Board, petition any United States district court within any district where the unfair labor practice in question has occurred, is alleged to have occurred, or wherein such person resides or transacts business, for appropriate injunctive relief pending the final adjudication of the Board with respect to such matter. Upon the filing of any such petition the district**

* The Norris-LaGuardia Act of 1932.

court shall have jurisdiction to grant such injunctive relief or temporary restraining order as it deems just and proper, notwithstanding any other provision of law: *Provided further*, That no temporary restraining order shall be issued without notice unless a petition alleges that substantial and irreparable injury to the charging party will be unavoidable and such temporary restraining order shall be effective for no longer than five days and will become void at the expiration of such period[.]: *Provided further, That such officer or regional attorney shall not apply for any restraining order under section 8(b)(7) if a charge against the employer under section 8(a)(2) has been filed and after the preliminary investigation, he has reasonable cause to believe that such charge is true and that a complaint should issue.* **Upon filing of any such petition the courts shall cause notice thereof to be served upon any person involved in the charge and such person, including the charging party, shall be given an opportunity to appear by counsel and present any relevant testimony: *Provided further*, That for the purposes of this subsection district courts shall be deemed to have jurisdiction of a labor organization (1) in the district in which such organization maintains its principal office, or (2) in any district in which its duly authorized officers or agents are engaged in promoting or protecting the interests of employee members. The service of legal process upon such officer or agent shall constitute service upon the labor organization and make such organization a party to the suit. In situations where such relief is appropriate the procedure specified herein shall apply to charges with respect to sections 8(b)(4)(D).**

(m) Whenever it is charged that any person has engaged in an unfair labor practice within the meaning of subsection (a)(3) or (b)(2) of section 8, such charge shall be given priority over all other cases except cases of like character in the office where it is filed or to which it is referred and cases given priority under subsection (l) of this section.

INVESTIGATORY POWERS

Sec. 11. For the purpose of all hearings and investigations, which, in the opinion of the Board, are necessary and proper for the exercise of the powers vested in it by section 9 and section 10—

(1) The Board, or its duly authorized agents or agencies, shall at all reasonable times have access to, for the purpose of examination, and the right to copy any evidence of any person being investigated or proceeded against that relates to any matter under investigation or in question. The Board, or any member thereof, shall upon application of any party to such proceedings, forthwith issue to such party subpoenas requiring the attendance and testimony of witnesses or the production of any evidence in such proceeding or investigation requested in such application. **Within five days after the service of a subpoena on any person**

requiring the production of any evidence in his possession or under his control, such person may petition the Board to revoke, and the Board shall revoke, such subpoena if in its opinion the evidence whose production is required does not relate to any matter under investigation, or any matter in question in such proceedings, or if in its opinion such subpoena does not describe with sufficient particularity the evidence whose production is required. Any member of the Board, or any agent or agency designated by the Board for such purposes, may administer oaths and affirmations, examine witnesses, and receive evidence. Such attendance of witnesses and the production of such evidence may be required from any place in the United States or any Territory or possession thereof, at any designated place of hearing.

(2) In case of contumacy or refusal to obey a subpoena issued to any person, any district court of the United States or the United States courts of any Territory or possession, or the District Court of the United States for the District of Columbia, within the jurisdiction of which the inquiry is carried on or within the jurisdiction of which said person guilty of contumacy or refusal to obey is found or resides or transacts business, upon application by the Board shall have jurisdiction to issue to such person an order requiring such person to appear before the Board, its member, agent, or agency, there to produce evidence if so ordered, or there to give testimony touching the matter under investigation or in question; and any failure to obey such order of the court may be punished by said court as a contempt thereof.

[(3) No person shall be excused from attending and testifying or from producing books, records, correspondence, documents, or other evidence in obedience to the subpoena of the Board, on the ground that the testimony or evidence required of him may tend to incriminate him or subject him to a penalty or forfeiture; but no individual shall be prosecuted or subjected to any penalty or forfeiture for or on account of any transaction, matter, or thing concerning which he is compelled, after having claimed his privilege against self-incrimination, to testify or produce evidence, except that such individual so testifying shall not be exempt from prosecution and punishment for perjury committed in so testifying.]*

(4) Complaints, orders, and other process and papers of the Board, its member, agent, or agency, may be served either personally or by registered mail or by telegraph or by leaving a copy thereof at the principal office or place of business of the person required to be served. The verified return by the individual so serving the same setting forth the manner of such service shall be proof of the same, and the return post office receipt or telegraph receipt therefor when registered and mailed or telegraphed as aforesaid shall be proof of service of the same. Witnesses

---

* Section 11(3) was repealed in 1970, by 84 Stat. 930. Similar immunity provisions were substituted; see 18 U.S.C. §§ 6001, 6002, 6004 (1970).

summoned before the Board, its member, agent, or agency, shall be paid the same fees and mileage that are paid witnesses in the courts of the United States, and witnesses whose depositions are taken and the persons taking the same shall severally be entitled to the same fees as are paid for like services in the courts of the United States.

(5) All process of any court to which application may be made under this Act may be served in the judicial district wherein the defendant or other person required to be served resides or may be found.

(6) The several departments and agencies of the Government, when directed by the President, shall furnish the Board, upon its request, all records, papers, and information in their possession relating to any matter before the Board.

Sec. 12. Any person who shall willfully resist, prevent, impede, or interfere with any member of the Board or any of its agents or agencies in the performance of duties pursuant to this Act shall be punished by a fine of not more than $5,000 or by imprisonment for not more than one year, or both.

LIMITATIONS

Sec. 13. Nothing in this Act, **except as specifically provided for herein,** shall be construed so as either to interfere with or impede or diminish in any way the right to strike, **or to affect the limitations or qualifications on that right.**

Sec. 14. (a) Nothing herein shall prohibit any individual employed as a supervisor from becoming or remaining a member of a labor organization, but no employer subject to this Act shall be compelled to deem individuals defined herein as supervisors as employees for the purpose of any law, either national or local, relating to collective bargaining.

(b) Nothing in this Act shall be construed as authorizing the execution or application of agreements requiring membership in a labor organization as a condition of employment in any State or Territory in which such execution or application is prohibited by State or Territorial law.

(c)(1) The Board, in its discretion, may, by rule of decision or by published rules adopted pursuant to the Administrative Procedure Act, decline to assert jurisdiction over any labor dispute involving any class or category of employers, where, in the opinion of the Board, the effect of such labor dispute on commerce is not sufficiently substantial to warrant the exercise of its jurisdiction: Provided, That the Board shall not decline to assert jurisdiction over any labor dispute over which it would assert jurisdiction under the standards prevailing upon August 1, 1959.

(2) Nothing in this Act shall be deemed to prevent or bar any agency or the courts of any State or Territory (including the Commonwealth of Puerto Rico, Guam, and the Virgin Islands), from assuming and asserting

jurisdiction over labor disputes over which the Board declines, pursuant to paragraph (1) of this subsection, to assert jurisdiction.

Sec. 15. [Reference to repealed provisions of the Bankruptcy Act.]

Sec. 16. If any provision of this Act, or the application of such provision to any person or circumstances, shall be held invalid, the remainder of this Act, or the application of such provision to persons or circumstances other than those as to which it is held invalid, shall not be affected thereby.

Sec. 17. This Act may be cited as the "National Labor Relations Act."

Sec. 18. [This section, which refers to the now-repealed Sections 9(f), (g), (h), is omitted.]

INDIVIDUALS WITH RELIGIOUS CONVICTIONS

Sec. 19. Any employee who is a member of and adheres to established and traditional tenets or teachings of a bona fide religion, body, or sect which has historically held conscientious objections to joining or financially supporting labor organizations shall not be required to join or financially support any labor organization as a condition of employment; except that such employee may be required in a contract between such employee's employer and a labor organization in lieu of periodic dues and initiation fees, to pay sums equal to such dues and initiation fees to a nonreligious, nonlabor organization charitable fund exempt from taxation under section 501(c)(3) of title 26 of the Internal Revenue Code [section 501(c)(3) of title 26], chosen by such employee from a list of at least three such funds, designated in such contract or if the contract fails to designate such funds, then to any such fund chosen by the employee. If such employee who holds conscientious objections pursuant to this section requests the labor organization to use the grievance-arbitration procedure on the employee's behalf, the labor organization is authorized to charge the employee for the reasonable cost of using such procedure.*

* This section was added by Pub.L. 93–360, July 26, 1974, 88 Stat. 397, and amended, Pub.L. 96–593, Dec. 24, 1980, 94 Stat. 3452.

LABOR MANAGEMENT RELATIONS ACT

61 Stat. 136 (1947), as amended; 29 U.S.C. §§ 141–97 (1988).

SHORT TITLE AND DECLARATION OF POLICY

Sec. 1. (a) This Act may be cited as the "Labor Management Relations Act, 1947."

(b) Industrial strife which interferes with the normal flow of commerce and with the full production of articles and commodities for commerce, can be avoided or substantially minimized if employers, employees, and labor organizations each recognize under law one another's legitimate rights in their relations with each other, and above all recognize under law that neither party has any right in its relations with any other to engage in acts or practices which jeopardize the public health, safety, or interest.

It is the purpose and policy of this Act, in order to promote the full flow of commerce, to prescribe the legitimate rights of both employees and employers in their relations affecting commerce, to provide orderly and peaceful procedures for preventing the interference by either with the legitimate rights of the other, to protect the rights of individual employees in their relations with labor organizations whose activities affect commerce, to define and proscribe practices on the part of labor and management which affect commerce and are inimical to the general welfare, and to protect the rights of the public in connection with labor disputes affecting commerce.

TITLE I

AMENDMENT OF NATIONAL LABOR RELATIONS ACT

Sec. 101. The National Labor Relations Act is hereby amended to read as follows: [The text of the National Labor Relations Act as amended is set forth supra.]

TITLE II

CONCILIATION OF LABOR DISPUTES IN INDUSTRIES AFFECTING COMMERCE; NATIONAL EMERGENCIES

Sec. 201. That it is the policy of the United States that—

(a) sound and stable industrial peace and the advancement of the general welfare, health, and safety of the Nation and of the best interests of employers and employees can most satisfactorily be secured by the settlement of issues between employers and employees through the processes of conference and collective bargaining between employers and the representatives of their employees;

(b) the settlement of issues between employers and employees through collective bargaining may be advanced by making available full and adequate governmental facilities for conciliation, mediation, and voluntary arbitration to aid and encourage employers and the representatives of their employees to reach and maintain agreements concerning rates of pay, hours, and working conditions, and to make all reasonable efforts to settle their differences by mutual agreement reached through conferences and collective bargaining or by such methods as may be provided for in any applicable agreement for the settlement of disputes; and

(c) certain controversies which arise between parties to collective-bargaining agreements may be avoided or minimized by making available full and adequate governmental facilities for furnishing assistance to employers and the representatives of their employees in formulating for inclusion within such agreements provision for adequate notice of any proposed changes in the terms of such agreements, for the final adjustment of grievances or questions regarding the application or interpretation of such agreements, and other provisions designed to prevent the subsequent arising of such controversies.

Sec. 202. (a) There is hereby created an independent agency to be known as the Federal Mediation and Conciliation Service (herein referred to as the "Service," except that for sixty days after the date of the enactment of this Act such term shall refer to the Conciliation Service of the Department of Labor). The Service shall be under the direction of a Federal Mediation and Conciliation Director (hereinafter referred to as the "Director"), who shall be appointed by the President by and with the advice and consent of the Senate. The Director shall not engage in any other business, vocation, or employment.

(b) The Director is authorized, subject to the civil-service laws, to appoint such clerical and other personnel as may be necessary for the execution of the functions of the Service, and shall fix their compensation in accordance with chapter 51 and subchapter III of chapter 53 of title 5, and may, without regard to the provisions of the civil-service laws, appoint such conciliators and mediators as may be necessary to carry out the functions of the Service. The Director is authorized to make such expenditures for supplies, facilities, and services as he deems necessary. Such expenditures shall be allowed and paid upon presentation of itemized vouchers therefor approved by the Director or by any employee designated by him for that purpose.

(c) The principal office of the Service shall be in the District of Columbia, but the Director may establish regional offices convenient to localities in which labor controversies are likely to arise. The Director may by order, subject to revocation at any time, delegate any authority and discretion conferred upon him by this Act to any regional director, or other officer or employee of the Service. The Director may establish suitable procedures for cooperation with State and local mediation agencies. The Director shall make an annual report in writing to Congress at the end of the fiscal year.

(d) All mediation and conciliation functions of the Secretary of Labor or the United States Conciliation Service under section 8 of the Act entitled "An Act to create a Department of Labor," approved March 4, 1913 (U.S.C., title 29, sec. 51), and all functions of the United States Conciliation Service under any other law are transferred to the Federal Mediation and Conciliation Service, together with the personnel and records of the United States Conciliation Service. Such transfer shall take effect upon the sixtieth day after June 23, 1947. Such transfer shall not affect any proceedings pending before the United States Conciliation Service or any certification, order, rule, or regulation theretofore made by it or by the Secretary of Labor. The Director and the Service shall not be subject in any way to the jurisdiction or authority of the Secretary of Labor or any official or division of the Department of Labor.

FUNCTIONS OF THE SERVICE

Sec. 203. (a) It shall be the duty of the Service, in order to prevent or minimize interruptions of the free flow of commerce growing out of labor disputes, to assist parties to labor disputes in industries affecting commerce to settle such disputes through conciliation and mediation.

(b) The Service may proffer its services in any labor dispute in any industry affecting commerce, either upon its own motion or upon the request of one or more of the parties to the dispute, whenever in its judgment such dispute threatens to cause a substantial interruption of commerce. The Director and the Service are directed to avoid attempting to mediate disputes which would have only a minor effect on interstate commerce if State or other conciliation services are available to the parties. Whenever the Service does proffer its services in any dispute, it shall be the duty of the Service promptly to put itself in communication with the parties and to use its best efforts, by mediation and conciliation, to bring them to agreement.

(c) If the Director is not able to bring the parties to agreement by conciliation within a reasonable time, he shall seek to induce the parties voluntarily to seek other means of settling the dispute without resort to strike, lock-out, or other coercion, including submission to the employees in the bargaining unit of the employer's last offer of settlement for approval or rejection in a secret ballot. The failure or refusal of either party to agree to any procedure suggested by the Director shall not be deemed a violation of any duty or obligation imposed by this Act.

(d) Final adjustment by a method agreed upon by the parties is hereby declared to be the desirable method for settlement of grievance disputes arising over the application or interpretation of an existing collective-bargaining agreement. The Service is directed to make its conciliation and mediation services available in the settlement of such grievance disputes only as a last resort and in exceptional cases.

(e)* The Service is authorized and directed to encourage and support the establishment and operation of joint labor management activities conducted by plant, area, and industrywide committees designed to improve labor management relationships, job security and organizational effectiveness, in accordance with the provisions of section 205A.

Sec. 204. (a) In order to prevent or minimize interruptions of the free flow of commerce growing out of labor disputes, employers and employees and their representatives, in any industry affecting commerce, shall—

(1) exert every reasonable effort to make and maintain agreements concerning rates of pay, hours, and working conditions, including provision for adequate notice of any proposed change in the terms of such agreements;

(2) whenever a dispute arises over the terms or application of a collective-bargaining agreement and a conference is requested by a party or prospective party thereto, arrange promptly for such a conference to be held and endeavor in such conference to settle such dispute expeditiously; and

(3) in case such dispute is not settled by conference, participate fully and promptly in such meetings as may be undertaken by the Service under this Act for the purpose of aiding in a settlement of the dispute.

Sec. 205. (a) There is created a National Labor-Management Panel which shall be composed of twelve members appointed by the President, six of whom shall be selected from among persons outstanding in the field of management and six of whom shall be selected from among persons outstanding in the field of labor. Each member shall hold office for a term of three years, except that any member appointed to fill a vacancy occurring prior to the expiration of the term for which his predecessor was appointed shall be appointed for the remainder of such term, and the terms of office of the members first taking office shall expire, as designated by the President at the time of appointment, four at the end of the first year, four at the end of the second year, and four at the end of the third year after the date of appointment. Members of the panel, when serving on business of the panel, shall be paid compensation at the rate of $25 per day, and shall also be entitled to receive an allowance for actual and necessary travel and subsistence expenses while so serving away from their places of residence.

(b) It shall be the duty of the panel, at the request of the Director, to advise in the avoidance of industrial controversies and the manner in

* Subsection (e) was added in 1978, by Pub.L. 95–524, § 6(c)(1), 92 Stat. 2020.

which mediation and voluntary adjustment shall be administered, particularly with reference to controversies affecting the general welfare of the country.

Sec. 205A.* **(a)**(1) The Service is authorized and directed to provide assistance in the establishment and operation of plant, area and industrywide labor management committees which—

(A) have been organized jointly by employers and labor organizations representing employees in that plant, area, or industry; and

(B) are established for the purpose of improving labor management relationships, job security, organizational effectiveness, enhancing economic development or involving workers in decisions affecting their jobs including improving communication with respect to subjects of mutual interest and concern.

(2) The Service is authorized and directed to enter into contracts and to make grants, where necessary or appropriate, to fulfill its responsibilities under this section.

(b)(1) No grant may be made, no contract may be entered into and no other assistance may be provided under the provisions of this section to a plant labor management committee unless the employees in that plant are represented by a labor organization and there is in effect at that plant a collective bargaining agreement.

(2) No grant may be made, no contract may be entered into and no other assistance may be provided under the provisions of this section to an area or industrywide labor management committee unless its participants include any labor organizations certified or recognized as the representative of the employees of an employer participating in such committee. Nothing in this clause shall prohibit participation in an area or industrywide committee by an employer whose employees are not represented by a labor organization.

(3) No grant may be made under the provisions of this section to any labor management committee which the Service finds to have as one of its purposes the discouragement of the exercise of rights contained in section 7 of the National Labor Relations Act (29 U.S.C. § 157) [section 157 of this title], or the interference with collective bargaining in any plant, or industry.

(c) The Service shall carry out the provisions of this section through an office established for that purpose.

(d) There are authorized to be appropriated to carry out the provisions of this section $10,000,000 for the fiscal year 1979, and such sums as may be necessary thereafter.

* This section was added in 1978, by Pub.L. 95–524, § 6(c)(2), 92 Stat. 2020.

NATIONAL EMERGENCIES

Sec. 206. Whenever in the opinion of the President of the United States, a threatened or actual strike or lock-out affecting an entire industry or a substantial part thereof engaged in trade, commerce, transportation, transmission, or communication among the several States or with foreign nations, or engaged in the production of goods for commerce, will, if permitted to occur or to continue, imperil the national health or safety, he may appoint a board of inquiry to inquire into the issues involved in the dispute and to make a written report to him within such time as he shall prescribe. Such report shall include a statement of the facts with respect to the dispute, including each party's statement of its position but shall not contain any recommendations. The President shall file a copy of such report with the Service and shall make its contents available to the public.

Sec. 207. (a) A board of inquiry shall be composed of a chairman and such other members as the President shall determine, and shall have power to sit and act in any place within the United States and to conduct such hearings either in public or in private, as it may deem necessary or proper, to ascertain the facts with respect to the causes and circumstances of the dispute.

(b) Members of a board of inquiry shall receive compensation at the rate of $50 for each day actually spent by them in the work of the board, together with necessary travel and subsistence expenses.

(c) For the purpose of any hearing or inquiry conducted by any board appointed under this title, the provisions of sections 9 and 10 (relating to the attendance of witnesses and the production of books, papers, and documents) of the Federal Trade Commission Act of September 16, 1914, as amended (U.S.C. 19, title 15, secs. 49 and 50, as amended), are made applicable to the powers and duties of such board.

Sec. 208. (a) Upon receiving a report from a board of inquiry the President may direct the Attorney General to petition any district court of the United States having jurisdiction of the parties to enjoin such strike or lock-out or the continuing thereof, and if the court finds that such threatened or actual strike or lock-out—

(i) affects an entire industry or a substantial part thereof engaged in trade, commerce, transportation, transmission, or communication among the several States or with foreign nations, or engaged in the production of goods for commerce; and

(ii) if permitted to occur or to continue, will imperil the national health or safety, it shall have jurisdiction to enjoin any such strike or lock-out, or the continuing thereof, and to make such other orders as may be appropriate.

(b) In any case, the provisions of the Act of March 23, 1932, entitled "An Act to amend the Judicial Code and to define and limit the jurisdiction of courts sitting in equity, and for other purposes," shall not be applicable.

(c) The order or orders of the court shall be subject to review by the appropriate United States court of appeals and by the Supreme Court upon writ of certiorari or certification as provided in sections 239 and 240 of the Judicial Code, as amended (U.S.C., title 29, secs. 346 and 347).

Sec. 209. (a) Whenever a district court has issued an order under section 208 enjoining acts or practices which imperil or threaten to imperil the national health or safety, it shall be the duty of the parties to the labor dispute giving rise to such order to make every effort to adjust and settle their differences, with the assistance of the Service created by this Act. Neither party shall be under any duty to accept, in whole or in part, any proposal of settlement made by the Service.

(b) Upon the issuance of such order, the President shall reconvene the board of inquiry which has previously reported with respect to the dispute. At the end of a sixty-day period (unless the dispute has been settled by that time), the board of inquiry shall report to the President the current position of the parties and the efforts which have been made for settlement, and shall include a statement by each party of its position and a statement of the employer's last offer of settlement. The President shall make such report available to the public. The National Labor Relations Board, within the succeeding fifteen days, shall take a secret ballot of the employees of each employer involved in the dispute on the question of whether they wish to accept the final offer of settlement made by their employer as stated by him and shall certify the results thereof to the Attorney General within five days thereafter.

Sec. 210. Upon the certification of the results of such ballot or upon a settlement being reached, whichever happens sooner, the Attorney General shall move the court to discharge the injunction, which motion shall then be granted and the injunction discharged. When such motion is granted, the President shall submit to the Congress a full and comprehensive report of the proceedings, including the findings of the board of inquiry and the ballot taken by the National Labor Relations Board, together with such recommendations as he may see fit to make for consideration and appropriate action.

COMPILATION OF COLLECTIVE BARGAINING AGREEMENTS, ETC.

Sec. 211. (a) For the guidance and information of interested representatives of employers, employees, and the general public, the Bureau of Labor Statistics of the Department of Labor shall maintain a file of copies of all available collective-bargaining agreements and other available agreements and actions thereunder settling or adjusting labor disputes. Such file shall be open to inspection under appropriate conditions prescribed by the Secretary of Labor, except that no specific information submitted in confidence shall be disclosed.

(b) The Bureau of Labor Statistics in the Department of Labor is authorized to furnish upon request of the Service, or employers, employees, or their representatives, all available data and factual information which may aid in the settlement of any labor dispute, except that no specific information submitted in confidence shall be disclosed.

EXEMPTION OF RAILWAY LABOR ACT

Sec. 212. The provisions of this title shall not be applicable with respect to any matter which is subject to the provisions of the Railway Labor Act, as amended from time to time.

CONCILIATION OF LABOR DISPUTES IN THE HEALTH CARE INDUSTRY

Sec. 213. (a) If, in the opinion of the Director of the Federal Mediation and Conciliation Service a threatened or actual strike or lockout affecting a health care institution will, if permitted to occur or to continue, substantially interrupt the delivery of health care in the locality concerned, the Director may further assist in the resolution of the impasse by establishing within 30 days after the notice to the Federal Mediation and Conciliation Service under clause (A) of the last sentence of section 8(d) (which is required by clause (3) of such section 8(d)), or within 10 days after the notice under clause (B), an impartial Board of Inquiry to investigate the issues involved in the dispute and to make a written report thereon to the parties within fifteen (15) days after the establishment of such a Board. The written report shall contain the findings of fact together with the Board's recommendations for settling the dispute, with the objective of achieving a prompt, peaceful and just settlement of the dispute. Each such Board shall be composed of such number of individuals as the Director may deem desirable. No member appointed under this section shall have any interest or involvement in the health care institutions or the employee organizations involved in the dispute.

(b)(1) Members of any board established under this section who are otherwise employed by the Federal Government shall serve without compensation but shall be reimbursed for travel, subsistence, and other necessary expenses incurred by them in carrying out its duties under this section.

(2) Members of any board established under this section who are not subject to paragraph (1) shall receive compensation at a rate prescribed by the Director but not to exceed the daily rate prescribed for GS-18 of the General Schedule under section 5332 of title 5, United States Code, including travel for each day they are engaged in the performance of their duties under this section and shall be entitled to reimbursement for travel, subsistence, and other necessary expenses incurred by them in carrying out their duties under this section.

(c) After the establishment of a board under subsection (a) of this section and for 15 days after any such board has issued its report, no change in the status quo in effect prior to the expiration of the contract in the case of negotiations for a contract renewal, or in effect prior to the time of the impasse in the case of an initial bargaining negotiation, except by agreement, shall be made by the parties to the controversy.

(d) There are authorized to be appropriated such sums as may be necessary to carry out the provisions of this section.

TITLE III

SUITS BY AND AGAINST LABOR ORGANIZATIONS

Sec. 301. (a) Suits for violation of contracts between an employer and a labor organization representing employees in an industry affecting commerce as defined in this Act, or between any such labor organizations, may be brought in any district court of the United States having jurisdiction of the parties, without respect to the amount in controversy or without regard to the citizenship of the parties.

(b) Any labor organization which represents employees in an industry affecting commerce as defined in this Act and any employer whose activities affect commerce as defined in this Act shall be bound by the acts of its agents. Any such labor organization may sue or be sued as an entity and in behalf of the employees whom it represents in the courts of the United States. Any money judgment against a labor organization in a district court of the United States shall be enforceable only against the organization as an entity and against its assets, and shall not be enforceable against any individual member or his assets.

(c) For the purposes of actions and proceedings by or against labor organizations in the district courts of the United States, district courts shall be deemed to have jurisdiction of a labor organization (1) in the district in which such organization maintains its principal office, or (2) in any district in which its duly authorized officers or agents are engaged in representing or acting for employee members.

(d) The service of summons, subpoena, or other legal process of any court of the United States upon an officer or agent of a labor organization, in his capacity as such, shall constitute service upon the labor organization.

(e) For the purposes of this section, in determining whether any person is acting as an "agent" of another person so as to make such other person responsible for his acts, the question of whether the specific acts performed were actually authorized or subsequently ratified shall not be controlling.

RESTRICTIONS ON PAYMENTS TO EMPLOYEE REPRESENTATIVES

Sec. 302. (a) It shall be unlawful for any employer or association of employers or any person who acts as a labor relations expert, adviser, or consultant to an employer or who acts in the interest of an employer to pay, lend, or deliver, or agree to pay, lend, or deliver, any money or other thing of value—

(1) to any representative of any of his employees who are employed in an industry affecting commerce; or

(2) to any labor organization, or any officer or employee thereof, which represents, seeks to represent, or would admit to membership, any of the employees of such employer who are employed in an industry affecting commerce; or

(3) to any employee or group or committee of employees of such employer employed in an industry affecting commerce in excess of their normal compensation for the purpose of causing such employee or group or committee directly or indirectly to influence any other employees in the exercise of the right to organize and bargain collectively through representatives of their own choosing; or

(4) to any officer or employee of a labor organization engaged in an industry affecting commerce with intent to influence him in respect to any of his actions, decisions, or duties as a representative of employees or as such officer or employee of such labor organization.

(b)(1) It shall be unlawful for any person to request, demand, receive, or accept, or agree to receive or accept, any payment, loan or delivery of any money or other thing of value prohibited by subsection (a).

(2) It shall be unlawful for any labor organization, or for any person acting as an officer, agent, representative, or employee of such labor organization, to demand or accept from the operator of any motor vehicle (as defined in part II of the Interstate Commerce Act) employed in the transportation of property in commerce, or the employer of any such operator, any money or other thing of value payable to such organization or to an officer, agent, representative or employee thereof as a fee or charge for the unloading, or in connection with the unloading, of the cargo of such vehicle: *Provided*, That nothing in this paragraph shall be construed to make unlawful any payment by an employer to any of his employees as compensation for their services as employees.

(c) The provisions of this section shall not be applicable (1) in respect to any money or other thing of value payable by an employer to any of his employees whose established duties include acting openly for such employer in matters of labor relations or personnel administration or to any representative of his employees, or to any officer or employee of a labor organization, who is also an employee or former employee of such employer, as compensation for, or by reason of, his service as an employee of such employer; (2) with respect to the payment or delivery of any money or other thing of value in satisfaction of a judgment of any court or a decision or award of an arbitrator or impartial chairman or in compromise, adjustment, settlement, or release of any claim, complaint, grievance, or dispute in the absence of fraud or duress; (3) with respect to the sale or purchase of an article or commodity at the prevailing market price in the regular course of business; (4) with respect to money deducted from the wages of employees in payment of membership dues in a labor organization: *Provided*, That the employer has received from each employee, on whose account such deductions are made, a written assignment which shall not be irrevocable for a period of more than one year, or beyond the termination date of the applicable collective agreement, whichever occurs sooner; (5) with respect to money or other thing of value paid to a trust fund established by such representative, for the sole and exclusive benefit of the employees of such employer, and their families and dependents (or of such employees, families, and dependents jointly with the employees of other employers making similar payments, and their families and dependents): *Provided*, That (A) such payments are held in trust for the purpose of paying, either from principal or income or both, for the benefit of employees, their families and dependents, for medical or hospital care, pensions on retirement or death of employees, compensation for injuries or illness resulting from occupational activity or insurance to provide any of the foregoing, or unemployment benefits or life insurance, disability and sickness insurance, or accident insurance; (B) the detailed basis on which such payments are to be made is specified in a written agreement with the employer, and employees and employers are equally represented in the administration of such fund, together with such neutral persons as the representatives of the employers and the representatives of employees may agree upon and in the event the employer and employee groups deadlock on the administration of such fund and there are no neutral persons empowered to break such deadlock, such agreement provides that the two groups shall agree on an impartial umpire to decide such dispute, or in event of their failure to agree within a reasonable length of time, an impartial umpire to decide such dispute shall, on petition of either group, be appointed by the district court of the United States for the district where the trust fund has its principal office, and shall also contain provisions for an annual audit of the trust fund, a statement of the results of which shall be available for inspection by interested persons at the principal office of the trust fund and at such other places as may be designated in such written agreement; and (C) such payments as are intended to be used for the purpose of providing pensions or annuities for employees are made to a separate trust which provides that the funds held therein cannot be used for any purpose other than paying such pensions or annuities; (6) with respect to money or other thing of value paid by any employer to a trust fund established by such representative for the purpose of pooled vacation, holiday, severance or similar benefits, or defraying costs of apprenticeship or other training programs: *Provided*, That the requirements of clause (B) of the proviso to clause (5) of this subsection, shall apply to such trust funds; (7) with respect to money or other thing of value paid by any employer to a pooled or individual trust fund established by such representative for the purpose of (A) scholarships for the benefit of employees, their families, and dependents for study at educational institutions, (B) child care centers for pre-school and school age dependents of employees, or (C) financial assistance for employee housing: *Provided,* That no labor organization or employer shall be required to bargain on the establishment of any such trust fund, and refusal to do so shall not constitute an unfair labor practice: *Provided further,* That the requirements of clause (B) of the proviso to clause (5) of this subsection shall apply to such trust funds; (8) with respect to money or any other thing of value paid by any employer to a trust fund established by such representative for the purpose of defraying the costs of legal services for employees, their families, and dependents for counsel or plan of their choice: *Provided,* That the requirements of clause (B) of the proviso to clause (5) of this subsection shall apply to such trust funds: *Provided further,* That no such legal services shall be furnished: (A) to initiate any proceeding directed (i) against any such employer or its officers or agents except in workman's compensation cases, or (ii) against such labor organization, or its parent or subordinate bodies, or their officers or agents, or (iii) against any other employer or labor organization, or their officers or agents, in any matter arising under the National Labor Relations Act, as amended, or this Act; and (B) in any proceeding where a labor organization would be prohibited from defraying the costs of legal services by the provisions of the Labor-Management Reporting and Disclosure Act of 1959; or (9) with respect to money or other things of value paid by an employer to a plant, area or industry-wide labor management committee established for one or more of the purposes set forth in section 5(b) of the Labor Management Cooperation Act of 1978.*

(d)(1) Any person who participates in a transaction involving a payment, loan, or delivery of money or other thing of value to a labor organization in payment of membership dues or to a joint labor-management trust fund as defined by clause (B) of the proviso to clause (5) of subsection (c) of this section or to a plant, area, or industry-wide labor-management committee that is received and used by such labor organization, trust fund, or committee, which transaction does not satisfy all the applicable requirements of subsections (c)(4) through (c)(9) of this section, and willfully and with intent to benefit himself or to benefit other persons he knows are not permitted to receive a payment, loan, money, or other thing of value under subsections (c)(4) through (c)(9) violates this subsection, shall, upon conviction thereof, be guilty of a felony and be subject to a fine of not more than $15,000, or imprisoned for not more than five years, or both; but if the value of the amount of money or thing of value involved in any violation of the provisions of this section does not exceed $1,000, such person shall be guilty of a misdemeanor and be

* Sec. 302(c)(7) was added by Pub.L. 91–86, Oct. 14, 1969, 83 Stat. 133; Sec. 302(c)(8) by Pub.L. 93–95, Aug. 15, 1973, 87 Stat. 314; and Sec. 302(c)(9) by Pub.L. 95–524, Oct. 27, 1978, 92 Stat. 2021.

subject to a fine of not more than $10,000, or imprisoned for not more than one year, or both.

(2) Except for violations involving transactions covered by subsection (d)(1) of this section, any person who willfully violates this section shall, upon conviction thereof, be guilty of a felony and be subject to a fine of not more than $15,000 or imprisoned for not more than five years, or both; but if the value of the amount of money or thing of value involved in any violation of the provisions of this section does not exceed $1,000, such person shall be guilty of a misdemeanor and be subject to a fine of not more than $10,000, or imprisoned for not more than one year, or both.*

(e) The district courts of the United States and the United States courts of the Territories and possessions shall have jurisdiction, for cause shown, and subject to the provisions of section 17 (relating to notice to opposite party) of the Act entitled "An Act to supplement existing laws against unlawful restraints and monopolies, and for other purposes," approved October 15, 1914, as amended (U.S.C., title 28, section 381), to restrain violations of this section, without regard to the provisions of sections 6 and 20 of such Act of October 15, 1914, as amended (U.S.C., title 15, section 17, and title 29, section 52), and the provisions of the Act entitled "An Act to amend the Judicial Code and to define and limit the jurisdiction of courts sitting in equity, and for other purposes," approved March 23, 1932 (U.S.C., title 29, sections 101–115).

(f) This section shall not apply to any contract in force on the date of enactment of this Act, until the expiration of such contract, or until July 1, 1948, whichever first occurs.

(g) Compliance with the restrictions contained in subsection (c)(5)(B) upon contributions to trust funds, otherwise lawful, shall not be applicable to contributions to such trust funds established by collective agreement prior to January 1, 1946, nor shall subsection (c)(5)(A) be construed as prohibiting contributions to such trust funds if prior to January 1, 1947, such funds contained provisions for pooled vacation benefits.

BOYCOTTS AND OTHER UNLAWFUL COMBINATIONS

Sec. 303. (a) It shall be unlawful, for the purpose of this section only, in an industry or activity affecting commerce, for any labor organization to engage in any activity or conduct defined as an unfair labor practice in section 8(b)(4) of the National Labor Relations Act, as amended.

(b) Whoever shall be injured in his business or property by reason of any violation of subsection (a) may sue therefor in any district court of the United States subject to the limitations and provisions of section 301 hereof without respect to the amount in controversy, or in any other court

* Section 302(d) was amended by Pub.L. 98–473, Oct. 12, 1984, 98 Stat. 2131.

having jurisdiction of the parties, and shall recover the damages by him sustained and the cost of the suit.

Sec. 304. [Repealed.]

Sec. 305. [Repealed.]

TITLE IV

CREATION OF JOINT COMMITTEE TO STUDY AND REPORT ON BASIC PROBLEMS AFFECTING FRIENDLY LABOR RELATIONS AND PRODUCTIVITY

* * *

TITLE V

DEFINITIONS

Sec. 501. When used in this Act—

(1) The term "industry affecting commerce" means any industry or activity in commerce or in which a labor dispute would burden or obstruct commerce or tend to burden or obstruct commerce or the free flow of commerce.

(2) The term "strike" includes any strike or other concerted stoppage of work by employees (including a stoppage by reason of the expiration of a collective-bargaining agreement) and any concerted slow-down or other concerted interruption of operations by employees.

(3) The terms "commerce", "labor disputes", "employer", "employee", "labor organization", "representative", "person", and "supervisor" shall have the same meaning as when used in the National Labor Relations Act as amended by this Act.

SAVING PROVISION

Sec. 502. Nothing in this Act shall be construed to require an individual employee to render labor or service without his consent, nor shall anything in this Act be construed to make the quitting of his labor by an individual employee an illegal act; nor shall any court issue any process to compel the performance by an individual employee of such labor or service, without his consent; nor shall the quitting of labor by an employee or employees in good faith because of abnormally dangerous conditions for work at the place of employment of such employee or employees be deemed a strike under this Act.

SEPARABILITY

Sec. 503. If any provision of this Act, or the application of such provision to any person or circumstance, shall be held invalid, the remainder of this Act, or the application of such provision to persons or circumstances other than those as to which it is held invalid, shall not be affected thereby.

LABOR-MANAGEMENT REPORTING AND DISCLOSURE ACT OF 1959

73 Stat. 519 (1959), as amended; 29 U.S.C. §§ 401–531 (1988).

SHORT TITLE

Sec. 1. This Act may be cited as the "Labor-Management Reporting and Disclosure Act of 1959".

DECLARATION OF FINDINGS, PURPOSES, AND POLICY

Sec. 2. (a) The Congress finds that, in the public interest, it continues to be the responsibility of the Federal Government to protect employees' rights to organize, choose their own representatives, bargain collectively, and otherwise engage in concerted activities for their mutual aid or protection; that the relations between employers and labor organizations and the millions of workers they represent have a substantial impact on the commerce of the Nation; and that in order to accomplish the objective of a free flow of commerce it is essential that labor organizations, employers, and their officials adhere to the highest standards of responsibility and ethical conduct in administering the affairs of their organizations, particularly as they affect labor-management relations.

(b) The Congress further finds, from recent investigations in the labor and management fields, that there have been a number of instances of breach of trust, corruption, disregard of the rights of individual employees, and other failures to observe high standards of responsibility and ethical conduct which require further and supplementary legislation that will afford necessary protection of the rights and interests of employees and the public generally as they relate to the activities of labor organizations, employers, labor relations consultants, and their officers and representatives.

(c) The Congress, therefore, further finds and declares that the enactment of this Act is necessary to eliminate or prevent improper practices on the part of labor organizations, employers, labor relations consultants, and their officers and representatives which distort and defeat the policies of the Labor Management Relations Act, 1947, as amended, and the Railway Labor Act, as amended, and have the tendency or necessary effect of burdening or obstructing commerce by (1) impairing the efficiency, safety, or operation of the instrumentalities of commerce; (2) occurring in the current of commerce; (3) materially affecting, restraining, or controlling the flow of raw materials or manufactured or processed goods into or from the channels of commerce, or the prices of such materials or goods in commerce; or (4) causing diminution of employment and wages in such volume as substantially to impair or disrupt the market for goods flowing into or from the channels of commerce.

DEFINITIONS

Sec. 3. For the purposes of titles I, II, III, IV, V (except section 505), and VI of this Act—

(a) "Commerce" means trade, traffic, commerce, transportation, transmission, or communication among the several States or between any State and any place outside thereof.

(b) "State" includes any State of the United States, the District of Columbia, Puerto Rico, the Virgin Islands, American Samoa, Guam, Wake Island, the Canal Zone, and Outer Continental Shelf lands defined in the Outer Continental Shelf Lands Act (43 U.S.C. §§ 1331–1343).

(c) "Industry affecting commerce" means any activity, business, or industry in commerce or in which a labor dispute would hinder or obstruct commerce or the free flow of commerce and includes any activity or industry "affecting commerce" within the meaning of the Labor Management Relations Act, 1947, as amended, or the Railway Labor Act, as amended.

(d) "Person" includes one or more individuals, labor organizations, partnerships, associations, corporations, legal representatives, mutual companies, joint-stock companies, trusts, unincorporated organizations, trustees, trustees in bankruptcy, or receivers.

(e) "Employer" means any employer or any group or association of employers engaged in an industry affecting commerce (1) which is, with respect to employees engaged in an industry affecting commerce, an employer within the meaning of any law of the United States relating to the employment of any employees or (2) which may deal with any labor organization concerning grievances, labor disputes, wages, rates of pay, hours of employment, or conditions of work, and includes any person acting directly or indirectly as an employer or as an agent of an employer in relation to an employee but does not include the United States or any corporation wholly owned by the Government of the United States or any State or political subdivision thereof.

(f) "Employee" means any individual employed by an employer, and includes any individual whose work has ceased as a consequence of, or in connection with, any current labor dispute or because of any unfair labor practice or because of exclusion or expulsion from a labor organization in any manner or for any reason inconsistent with the requirements of this Act.

(g) "Labor dispute" includes any controversy concerning terms, tenure, or conditions of employment, or concerning the association or representation of persons in negotiating, fixing, maintaining, changing or seeking to arrange terms or conditions of employment, regardless of whether the disputants stand in the proximate relation of employer and employee.

(h) "Trusteeship" means any receivership, trusteeship, or other method of supervision or control whereby a labor organization suspends the autonomy otherwise available to a subordinate body under its constitution or bylaws.

(i) "Labor organization" means a labor organization engaged in an industry affecting commerce and includes any organization of any kind, any agency, or employee representation committee, group, association, or plan so engaged in which employees participate and which exists for the purpose, in whole or in part, of dealing with employers concerning grievances, labor disputes, wages, rates of pay, hours, or other terms or conditions of employment, and any conference, general committee, joint or system board, or joint council so engaged which is subordinate to a national or international labor organization, other than a State or local central body.

(j) A labor organization shall be deemed to be engaged in an industry affecting commerce if it—

(1) is the certified representative of employees under the provisions of the National Labor Relations Act, as amended, or the Railway Labor Act, as amended; or

(2) although not certified, is a national or international labor organization or a local labor organization recognized or acting as the representative of employees of an employer or employers engaged in an industry affecting commerce; or

(3) has chartered a local labor organization or subsidiary body which is representing or actively seeking to represent employees of employers within the meaning of paragraph (1) or (2); or

(4) has been chartered by a labor organization representing or actively seeking to represent employees within the meaning of paragraph (1) or (2) as the local or subordinate body through which such employees may enjoy membership or become affiliated with such labor organization; or

(5) is a conference, general committee, joint or system board, or joint council, subordinate to a national or international labor organization, which includes a labor organization engaged in an industry affecting commerce within the meaning of any of the preceding paragraphs of this subsection, other than a State or local central body.

(k) "Secret ballot" means the expression by ballot, voting machine, or otherwise, but in no event by proxy, of a choice with respect to any election or vote taken upon any matter, which is cast in such a manner that the person expressing such choice cannot be identified with the choice expressed.

(*l*) "Trust in which a labor organization is interested" means a trust or other fund or organization (1) which was created or established by a labor organization, or one or more of the trustees or one or more members of the governing body of which is selected or appointed by a labor organization, and (2) a primary purpose of which is to provide benefits for the members of such labor organization or their beneficiaries.

(m) "Labor relations consultant" means any person who, for compensation, advises or represents an employer, employer organization, or labor organization concerning employee organizing, concerted activities, or collective bargaining activities.

(n) "Officer" means any constitutional officer, any person authorized to perform the functions of president, vice president, secretary, treasurer, or other executive functions of a labor organization, and any member of its executive board or similar governing body.

(*o*) "Member" or "member in good standing", when used in reference to a labor organization, includes any person who has fulfilled the requirements for membership in such organization, and who neither has voluntarily withdrawn from membership nor has been expelled or suspended from membership after appropriate proceedings consistent with lawful provisions of the constitution and bylaws of such organization.

(p) "Secretary" means the Secretary of Labor.

(q) "Officer, agent, shop steward, or other representative", when used with respect to a labor organization, includes elected officials and key administrative personnel, whether elected or appointed (such as business agents, heads of departments or major units, and organizers who exercise substantial independent authority), but does not include salaried nonsupervisory professional staff, stenographic, and service personnel.

(r) "District court of the United States" means a United States district court and a United States court of any place subject to the jurisdiction of the United States.

TITLE I—BILL OF RIGHTS OF MEMBERS OF LABOR ORGANIZATIONS

BILL OF RIGHTS

Sec. 101. (a)(1) EQUAL RIGHTS.—Every member of a labor organization shall have equal rights and privileges within such organization to nominate candidates, to vote in elections or referendums of the labor organization, to attend membership meetings, and to participate in the deliberations and voting upon the business of such meetings, subject to reasonable rules and regulations in such organization's constitution and bylaws.

(2) FREEDOM OF SPEECH AND ASSEMBLY.—Every member of any labor organization shall have the right to meet and assemble freely with other members; and to express any views, arguments, or opinions; and to express at meetings of the labor organization his views, upon

candidates in an election of the labor organization or upon any business properly before the meeting, subject to the organization's established and reasonable rules pertaining to the conduct of meetings: *Provided*, That nothing herein shall be construed to impair the right of a labor organization to adopt and enforce reasonable rules as to the responsibility of every member toward the organization as an institution and to his refraining from conduct that would interfere with its performance of its legal or contractual obligations.

(3) DUES, INITIATION FEES, AND ASSESSMENTS.—Except in the case of a federation of national or international labor organizations, the rates of dues and initiation fees payable by members of any labor organization in effect on the date of enactment of this Act shall not be increased, and no general or special assessment shall be levied upon such members, except—

(A) in a case of a local labor organization, (i) by majority vote by secret ballot of the members in good standing voting at a general or special membership meeting, after reasonable notice of the intention to vote upon such question, or (ii) by majority vote of the members in good standing voting in a membership referendum conducted by secret ballot; or

(B) in the case of a labor organization, other than a local labor organization or a federation of national or international labor organizations, (i) by majority vote of the delegates voting at a regular convention, or at a special convention of such labor organization held upon not less than thirty days' written notice to the principal office of each local or constituent labor organization entitled to such notice, or (ii) by majority vote of the members in good standing of such labor organization voting in a membership referendum conducted by secret ballot, or (iii) by majority vote of the members of the executive board or similar governing body of such labor organization, pursuant to express authority contained in the constitution and bylaws of such labor organization: *Provided*, That such action on the part of the executive board or similar governing body shall be effective only until the next regular convention of such labor organization.

(4) PROTECTION OF THE RIGHT TO SUE.—No labor organization shall limit the right of any member thereof to institute an action in any court, or in a proceeding before any administrative agency, irrespective of whether or not the labor organization or its officers are named as defendants or respondents in such action or proceeding, or the right of any member of a labor organization to appear as a witness in any judicial, administrative, or legislative proceeding, or to petition any legislature or to communicate with any legislator: *Provided*, That any such member may be required to exhaust reasonable hearing procedures (but not to exceed a four-month lapse of time) within such organization, before instituting legal or administrative proceedings against such organizations or any officer thereof: *And provided further*, That no

interested employer or employer association shall directly or indirectly finance, encourage, or participate in, except as a party, any such action, proceeding, appearance, or petition.

(5) SAFEGUARDS AGAINST IMPROPER DISCIPLINARY ACTION.—No member of any labor organization may be fined, suspended, expelled, or otherwise disciplined except for nonpayment of dues by such organization or by any officer thereof unless such member has been (A) served with written specific charges; (B) given a reasonable time to prepare his defense; (C) afforded a full and fair hearing.

(b) Any provision of the constitution and bylaws of any labor organization which is inconsistent with the provisions of this section shall be of no force or effect.

CIVIL ENFORCEMENT

Sec. 102. Any person whose rights secured by the provisions of this title have been infringed by any violation of this title may bring a civil action in a district court of the United States for such relief (including injunctions) as may be appropriate. Any such action against a labor organization shall be brought in the district court of the United States for the district where the alleged violation occurred, or where the principal office of such labor organization is located.

RETENTION OF EXISTING RIGHTS

Sec. 103. Nothing contained in this title shall limit the rights and remedies of any member of a labor organization under any State or Federal law or before any court or other tribunal, or under the constitution and bylaws of any labor organization.

RIGHT TO COPIES OF COLLECTIVE BARGAINING AGREEMENTS

Sec. 104. It shall be the duty of the secretary or corresponding principal officer of each labor organization, in the case of a local labor organization, to forward a copy of each collective bargaining agreement made by such labor organization with any employer to any employee who requests such a copy and whose rights as such employee are directly affected by such agreement, and in the case of a labor organization other than a local labor organization, to forward a copy of any such agreement to each constituent unit which has members directly affected by such agreement; and such officer shall maintain at the principal office of the labor organization of which he is an officer copies of any such agreement made or received by such labor organization, which copies shall be available for inspection by any member or by any employee whose rights are affected by such agreement. The provisions of section 210 shall be applicable in the enforcement of this section.

INFORMATION AS TO ACT

Sec. 105. Every labor organization shall inform its members concerning the provisions of this Act.

TITLE II—REPORTING BY LABOR ORGANIZATIONS, OFFICERS AND EMPLOYEES OF LABOR ORGANIZATIONS, AND EMPLOYERS

REPORT OF LABOR ORGANIZATIONS

Sec. 201. (a) Every labor organization shall adopt a constitution and bylaws and shall file a copy thereof with the Secretary, together with a report, signed by its president and secretary or corresponding principal officers, containing the following information—

(1) the name of the labor organization, its mailing address, and any other address at which it maintains its principal office or at which it keeps the records referred to in this title;

(2) the name and title of each of its officers;

(3) the initiation fee or fees required from a new or transferred member and fees for work permits required by the reporting labor organization;

(4) the regular dues or fees or other periodic payments required to remain a member of the reporting labor organization; and

(5) detailed statements, or references to specific provisions of documents filed under this subsection which contain such statements, showing the provision made and procedures followed with respect to each of the following: (A) qualifications for or restrictions on membership, (B) levying of assessments, (C) participation in insurance or other benefit plans, (D) authorization for disbursement of funds of the labor organization, (E) audit of financial transactions of the labor organization, (F) the calling of regular and special meetings, (G) the selection of officers and stewards and of any representatives to other bodies composed of labor organizations' representatives, with a specific statement of the manner in which each officer was elected, appointed, or otherwise selected, (H) discipline or removal of officers or agents for breaches of their trust, (I) imposition of fines, suspensions and expulsions of members, including the grounds for such action and any provision made for notice, hearing, judgment on the evidence, and appeal procedures, (J) authorization for bargaining demands, (K) ratification of contract terms, (L) authorization for strikes, and (M) issuance of work permits. Any change in the information required by this subsection shall be reported to the Secretary at the time the reporting labor organization files with the Secretary the annual financial report required by subsection (b).

(b) Every labor organization shall file annually with the Secretary a financial report signed by its president and treasurer or corresponding principal officers containing the following information in such detail as may be necessary accurately to disclose its financial condition and operations for its preceding fiscal year—

(1) assets and liabilities at the beginning and end of the fiscal year;

(2) receipts of any kind and the sources thereof;

(3) salary, allowances, and other direct or indirect disbursements (including reimbursed expenses) to each officer and also to each employee who, during such fiscal year, received more than $10,000 in the aggregate from such labor organization and any other labor organization affiliated with it or with which it is affiliated, or which is affiliated with the same national or international labor organization;

(4) direct and indirect loans made to any officer, employee, or member, which aggregated more than $250 during the fiscal year, together with a statement of the purpose, security, if any, and arrangements for repayment;

(5) direct and indirect loans to any business enterprise, together with a statement of the purpose, security, if any, and arrangements for repayment; and

(6) other disbursements made by it including the purposes thereof;

all in such categories as the Secretary may prescribe.

(c) Every labor organization required to submit a report under this title shall make available the information required to be contained in such report to all of its members, and every such labor organization and its officers shall be under a duty enforceable at the suit of any member of such organization in any State court of competent jurisdiction or in the district court of the United States for the district in which such labor organization maintains its principal office, to permit such member for just cause to examine any books, records, and accounts necessary to verify such report. The court in such action may, in its discretion, in addition to any judgment awarded to the plaintiff or plaintiffs, allow a reasonable attorney's fee to be paid by the defendant, and costs of the action.

REPORT OF OFFICERS AND EMPLOYEES OF LABOR ORGANIZATIONS

Sec. 202. (a) Every officer of a labor organization and every employee of a labor organization (other than an employee performing exclusively clerical or custodial services) shall file with the Secretary a signed report listing and describing for his preceding fiscal year—

(1) any stock, bond, security, or other interest, legal or equitable, which he or his spouse or minor child directly or indirectly held in, and any income or any other benefit with monetary value (including reimbursed expenses) which he or his spouse or minor child derived directly or indirectly from, an employer whose employees such labor organization represents or is actively seeking

to represent, except payments and other benefits received as a bona fide employee of such employer;

(2) any transaction in which he or his spouse or minor child engaged, directly or indirectly, involving any stock, bond, security, or loan to or from, or other legal or equitable interest in the business of an employer whose employees such labor organization represents or is actively seeking to represent;

(3) any stock, bond, security, or other interest, legal or equitable, which he or his spouse or minor child directly or indirectly held in, and any income or any other benefit with monetary value (including reimbursed expenses) which he or his spouse or minor child directly or indirectly derived from, any business a substantial part of which consists of buying from, selling or leasing to, or otherwise dealing with, the business of an employer whose employees such labor organization represents or is actively seeking to represent;

(4) any stock, bond, security, or other interest, legal or equitable, which he or his spouse or minor child directly or indirectly held in, and any income or any other benefit with monetary value (including reimbursed expenses) which he or his spouse or minor child directly or indirectly derived from, a business any part of which consists of buying from, or selling or leasing directly or indirectly to, or otherwise dealing with such labor organization;

(5) any direct or indirect business transaction or arrangement between him or his spouse or minor child and any employer whose employees his organization represents or is actively seeking to represent, except work performed and payments and benefits received as a bona fide employee of such employer and except purchases and sales of goods or services in the regular course of business at prices generally available to any employee of such employer; and

(6) any payment of money or other thing of value (including reimbursed expenses) which he or his spouse or minor child received directly or indirectly from any employer or any person who acts as a labor relations consultant to an employer, except payments of the kinds referred to in section 302(c) of the Labor Management Relations Act, 1947, as amended.

(b) The provisions of paragraphs (1), (2), (3), (4), and (5) of subsection (a) shall not be construed to require any such officer or employee to report his bona fide investments in securities traded on a securities exchange registered as a national securities exchange under the Securities Exchange Act of 1934, in shares in an investment company registered under the Investment Company Act of 1940, or in securities of a public utility holding company registered under the Public Utility Holding Company Act of 1935, or to report any income derived therefrom.

(c) Nothing contained in this section shall be construed to require any officer or employee of a labor organization to file a report under subsection (a) unless he or his spouse or minor child holds or has held an interest, has received income or any other benefit with monetary value or a loan, or has engaged in a transaction described therein.

REPORT OF EMPLOYERS

Sec. 203. (a) Every employer who in any fiscal year made—

(1) any payment or loan, direct or indirect, of money or other thing of value (including reimbursed expenses), or any promise or agreement therefor, to any labor organization or officer, agent, shop steward, or other representative of a labor organization, or employee of any labor organization, except (A) payments or loans made by any national or State bank, credit union, insurance company, savings and loan association or other credit institution and (B) payments of the kind referred to in section 302(c) of the Labor Management Relations Act, 1947, as amended;

(2) any payment (including reimbursed expenses) to any of his employees, or any group or committee of such employees, for the purpose of causing such employee or group or committee of employees to persuade other employees to exercise or not to exercise, or as the manner of exercising, the right to organize and bargain collectively through representatives of their own choosing unless such payments were contemporaneously or previously disclosed to such other employees;

(3) any expenditure, during the fiscal year, where an object thereof, directly or indirectly, is to interfere with, restrain, or coerce employees in the exercise of the right to organize and bargain collectively through representatives of their own choosing, or is to obtain information concerning the activities of employees or a labor organization in connection with a labor dispute involving such employer, except for use solely in conjunction with an administrative or arbitral proceeding or a criminal or civil judicial proceeding;

(4) any agreement or arrangement with a labor relations consultant or other independent contractor or organization pursuant to which such person undertakes activities where an object thereof, directly or indirectly, is to persuade employees to exercise or not to exercise, or persuade employees as to the manner of exercising, the right to organize and bargain collectively through representatives of their own choosing, or undertakes to supply such employer with information concerning the activities of employees or a labor organization in connection with a labor dispute involving such employer, except information for use solely in conjunction with an administrative or arbitral proceeding or a criminal or civil judicial proceeding; or

(5) any payment (including reimbursed expenses) pursuant to an agreement or arrangement described in subdivision (4);

shall file with the Secretary a report, in a form prescribed by him, signed by its president and treasurer or corresponding principal officers showing in detail the date and amount of each such payment, loan, promise, agreement, or arrangement and the name, address, and position, if any, in any firm or labor organization of the person to whom it was made and a full explanation of the circumstances of all such payments, including the terms of any agreement or understanding pursuant to which they were made.

(b) Every person who pursuant to any agreement or arrangement with an employer undertakes activities where an object thereof is, directly or indirectly—

(1) to persuade employees to exercise or not to exercise, or persuade employees as to the manner of exercising, the right to organize and bargain collectively through representatives of their own choosing; or

(2) to supply an employer with information concerning the activities of employees or a labor organization in connection with a labor dispute involving such employer, except information for use solely in conjunction with an administrative or arbitral proceeding or a criminal or civil judicial proceeding;

shall file within thirty days after entering into such agreement or arrangement a report with the Secretary, signed by its president and treasurer or corresponding principal officers, containing the name under which such person is engaged in doing business and the address of its principal office, and a detailed statement of the terms and conditions of such agreement or arrangement. Every such person shall file annually, with respect to each fiscal year during which payments were made as a result of such an agreement or arrangement, a report with the Secretary, signed by its president and treasurer or corresponding principal officers, containing a statement (A) of its receipts of any kind from employers on account of labor relations advice or services, designating the sources thereof, and (B) of its disbursements of any kind, in connection with such services and the purposes thereof. In each such case such information shall be set forth in such categories as the Secretary may prescribe.

(c) Nothing in this section shall be construed to require any employer or other person to file a report covering the services of such person by reason of his giving or agreeing to give advice to such employer or representing or agreeing to represent such employer before any court, administrative agency, or tribunal of arbitration or engaging or agreeing to engage in collective bargaining on behalf of such employer with respect to wages, hours, or other terms or conditions of employment or the negotiation of an agreement or any question arising thereunder.

(d) Nothing contained in this section shall be construed to require an employer to file a report under subsection (a) unless he has made an expenditure, payment, loan, agreement, or arrangement of the kind described therein. Nothing contained in this section shall be construed to require any other person to file a report under subsection (b) unless he was a party to an agreement or arrangement of the kind described therein.

(e) Nothing contained in this section shall be construed to require any regular officer, supervisor, or employee of an employer to file a report in connection with services rendered to such employer nor shall any employer be required to file a report covering expenditures made to any regular officer, supervisor, or employee of an employer as compensation for service as a regular officer, supervisor, or employee of such employer.

(f) Nothing contained in this section shall be construed as an amendment to, or modification of the rights protected by, section 8(c) of the National Labor Relations Act, as amended.

(g) The term "interfere with, restrain, or coerce" as used in this section means interference, restraint, and coercion which, if done with respect to the exercise of rights guaranteed in section 7 of the National Labor Relations Act, as amended, would, under section 8(a) of such Act, constitute an unfair labor practice.

ATTORNEY-CLIENT COMMUNICATIONS EXEMPTED

Sec. 204. Nothing contained in this Act shall be construed to require an attorney who is a member in good standing of the bar of any State, to include in any report required to be filed pursuant to the provisions of this Act any information which was lawfully communicated to such attorney by any of his clients in the course of a legitimate attorney-client relationship.

REPORTS MADE PUBLIC INFORMATION

Sec. 205. (a) The contents of the reports and documents filed with the Secretary pursuant to sections 201, 202, 203, and 211 shall be public information, and the Secretary may publish any information and data which he obtains pursuant to the provisions of this title. The Secretary may use the information and data for statistical and research purposes, and compile and publish such studies, analyses, reports, and surveys based thereon as he may deem appropriate.

(b) The Secretary shall by regulation make reasonable provision for the inspection and examination, on the request of any person, of the information and data contained in any report or other document filed with him pursuant to section 201, 202, 203, or 211.

(c) The Secretary shall by regulation provide for the furnishing by the Department of Labor of copies of reports or other documents filed with the Secretary pursuant to this title, upon payment of a charge based upon the cost of the service. The Secretary shall make available without payment of a charge, or require any person to furnish, to such State agency as is designated by law or by the Governor of the State in which such person has his principal place of business or headquarters, upon request of the Governor of such State, copies of any reports and documents filed by such person with the Secretary pursuant to section 201, 202, 203, or 211, or of information and data contained therein. No person shall be required by reason of any law of any State to furnish to any officer or agency of such State any information included in a report filed by such person with the Secretary pursuant to the provisions of this title, if a copy of such report, or of the portion thereof containing such information, is furnished to such officer or agency. All moneys received in payment of such charges fixed by the Secretary pursuant to this subsection shall be deposited in the general fund of the Treasury.

RETENTION OF RECORDS

Sec. 206. Every person required to file any report under this title shall maintain records on the matters required to be reported which will provide in sufficient detail the necessary basic information and data from which the documents filed with the Secretary may be verified, explained or clarified, and checked for accuracy and completeness, and shall include vouchers, worksheets, receipts, and applicable resolutions, and shall keep such records available for examination for a period of not less than five years after the filing of the documents based on the information which they contain.

EFFECTIVE DATE

Sec. 207. (a) Each labor organization shall file the initial report required under section 201(a) within ninety days after the date on which it first becomes subject to this Act.

(b) Each person required to file a report under section 201(b), 202, 203(a), or the second sentence of 203(b), or section 211 shall file such report within ninety days after the end of each of its fiscal years; except that where such person is subject to section 201(b), 202, 203(a), the second sentence of 203(b), or section 211, as the case may be, for only a portion of such a fiscal year (because the date of enactment of this Act occurs during such person's fiscal year or such person becomes subject to this Act during its fiscal year) such person may consider that portion as the entire fiscal year in making such report.

RULES AND REGULATIONS

Sec. 208. The Secretary shall have authority to issue, amend, and rescind rules and regulations prescribing the form and publication of reports required to be filed under this title and such other reasonable rules and regulations (including rules prescribing reports concerning trusts in which a labor organization is interested) as he may find necessary to prevent the circumvention or evasion of such reporting requirements. In exercising his power under this section the Secretary shall prescribe by general rule simplified reports for labor organizations or employers for whom he finds that by virtue of their size a detailed report would be unduly burdensome, but the Secretary may revoke such provision for simplified forms of any labor organization or employer if he determines, after such investigation as he deems proper and due notice and opportunity for a hearing, that the purposes of this section would be served thereby.

CRIMINAL PROVISIONS

Sec. 209. (a) Any person who willfully violates this title shall be fined not more than $10,000 or imprisoned for not more than one year, or both.

(b) Any person who makes a false statement or representation of a material fact, knowing it to be false, or who knowingly fails to disclose a material fact, in any document, report, or other information required under the provisions of this title shall be fined not more than $10,000 or imprisoned for not more than one year, or both.

(c) Any person who willfully makes a false entry in or willfully conceals, withholds, or destroys any books, records, reports, or statements required to be kept by any provision of this title shall be fined not more than $10,000 or imprisoned for not more than one year, or both.

(d) Each individual required to sign reports under sections 201 and 203 shall be personally responsible for the filing of such reports and for any statement contained therein which he knows to be false.

CIVIL ENFORCEMENT

Sec. 210. Whenever it shall appear that any person has violated or is about to violate any of the provisions of this title, the Secretary may bring a civil action for such relief (including injunctions) as may be appropriate. Any such action may be brought in the district court of the United States where the violation occurred or, at the option of the parties, in the United States District Court for the District of Columbia.

SURETY COMPANY REPORTS

Sec. 211. Each surety company which issues any bond required by this Act or the Employee Retirement Income Security Act of 1974 shall file annually with the Secretary, with respect to each fiscal year during which any such bond was in force, a report, in such form and detail as he may prescribe by regulation, filed by the president and treasurer or corresponding principal officers of the surety company, describing its bond experience under each such Act, including information as to the premiums received, total claims paid, amounts recovered by way of subrogation, administrative and legal expenses and such related data and information as the Secretary shall determine to be necessary in the public interest and to carry out the policy of the Act. Notwithstanding the foregoing, if the Secretary finds that any such specific information cannot be practicably ascertained or would be uninformative, the Secretary may modify or waive the requirement for such information.

TITLE III—TRUSTEESHIPS

REPORTS

Sec. 301. (a) Every labor organization which has or assumes trusteeship over any subordinate labor organization shall file with the Secretary within thirty days after the date of the enactment of this Act or the imposition of any such trusteeship, and semiannually thereafter, a report, signed by its president and treasurer or corresponding principal officers, as well as by the trustees of such subordinate labor organization, containing the following information: (1) the name and address of the subordinate organization; (2) the date of establishing the trusteeship; (3) a detailed statement of the reason or reasons for establishing or continuing the trusteeship; and (4) the nature and extent of participation by the membership of the subordinate organization in the selection of delegates to represent such organization in regular or special conventions or other policy-determining bodies and in the election of officers of the labor organization which has assumed trusteeship over such subordinate organization. The initial report shall also include a full and complete account of the financial condition of such subordinate organization as of the time trusteeship was assumed over it. During the continuance of a trusteeship the labor organization which has assumed trusteeship over a subordinate labor organization shall file on behalf of the subordinate labor organization the annual financial report required by section 201(b) signed by the president and treasurer or corresponding principal officers of the labor organization which has assumed such trusteeship and the trustees of the subordinate labor organization.

(b) The provisions of sections 201(c), 205, 206, 208, and 210 shall be applicable to reports filed under this title.

(c) Any person who willfully violates this section shall be fined not more than $10,000 or imprisoned for not more than one year, or both.

(d) Any person who makes a false statement or representation of a material fact, knowing it to be false, or who knowingly fails to disclose a material fact, in any report required under the provisions of this section or willfully makes any false entry in or willfully withholds, conceals, or destroys any documents, books, records, reports, or statements upon which such report is based, shall be fined not more than $10,000 or imprisoned for not more than one year, or both.

(e) Each individual required to sign a report under this section shall be personally responsible for the filing of such report and for any statement contained therein which he knows to be false.

PURPOSES FOR WHICH A TRUSTEESHIP MAY BE ESTABLISHED

Sec. 302. Trusteeships shall be established and administered by a labor organization over a subordinate body only in accordance with the constitution and bylaws of the organization which has assumed trusteeship over the subordinate body and for the purpose of correcting corruption or financial malpractice, assuring the performance of collective bargaining agreements or other duties of a bargaining representative, restoring democratic procedures, or otherwise carrying out the legitimate objects of such labor organization.

UNLAWFUL ACTS RELATING TO LABOR ORGANIZATION UNDER TRUSTEESHIP

Sec. 303. (a) During any period when a subordinate body of a labor organization is in trusteeship, it shall be unlawful (1) to count the vote of delegates from such body in any convention or election of officers of the labor organization unless the delegates have been chosen by secret ballot in an election in which all the members in good standing of such subordinate body were eligible to participate, or (2) to transfer to such organization any current receipts or other funds of the subordinate body except the normal per capita tax and assessments payable by subordinate bodies not in trusteeship: *Provided*, That nothing herein contained shall prevent the distribution of the assets of a labor organization in accordance with its constitution and bylaws upon the bona fide dissolution thereof.

(b) Any person who willfully violates this section shall be fined not more than $10,000 or imprisoned for not more than one year, or both.

ENFORCEMENT

Sec. 304. (a) Upon the written complaint of any member or subordinate body of a labor organization alleging that such organization has violated the provisions of this title (except section 301) the Secretary shall investigate the complaint and if the Secretary finds probable cause to believe that such violation has occurred and has not been remedied he shall, without disclosing the identity of the complainant, bring a civil action in any district court of the United States having jurisdiction of the labor organization for such relief (including injunctions) as may be appropriate. Any member or subordinate body of a labor organization affected by any violation of this title (except section 301) may bring a civil action in any district court of the United States having jurisdiction of the labor organization for such relief (including injunctions) as may be appropriate.

(b) For the purpose of actions under this section, district courts of the United States shall be deemed to have jurisdiction of a labor organization (1) in the district in which the principal office of such labor organization is located, or (2) in any district in which its duly authorized officers or agents are engaged in conducting the affairs of the trusteeship.

(c) In any proceeding pursuant to this section a trusteeship established by a labor organization in conformity with the procedural requirements of its constitution and bylaws and authorized or ratified after a fair hearing either before the executive board or before such other body as may be provided in accordance with its constitution or bylaws shall be presumed valid for a period of eighteen months from the date of its establishment and shall not be subject to attack during such period except upon clear and convincing proof that the trusteeship was not established or maintained in good faith for a purpose allowable under section 302. After the expiration of eighteen months the trusteeship shall be presumed invalid in any such proceeding and its discontinuance shall be decreed unless the labor organization shall show by clear and convincing proof that the continuation of the trusteeship is necessary for a purpose allowable under section 302. In the latter event the court may dismiss the complaint or retain jurisdiction of the cause on such conditions and for such period as it deems appropriate.

REPORT TO CONGRESS

Sec. 305. The Secretary shall submit to the Congress at the expiration of three years from the date of enactment of this Act a report upon the operation of this title.

COMPLAINT BY SECRETARY

Sec. 306. The rights and remedies provided by this title shall be in addition to any and all other rights and remedies at law or in equity: *Provided,* That upon the filing of a complaint by the Secretary the jurisdiction of the district court over such trusteeship shall be exclusive and the final judgment shall be res judicata.

TITLE IV—ELECTIONS

TERMS OF OFFICE; ELECTION PROCEDURES

Sec. 401. (a) Every national or international labor organization, except a federation of national or international labor organizations, shall elect its officers not less often than once every five years either by secret ballot among the members in good standing or at a convention of delegates chosen by secret ballot.

(b) Every local labor organization shall elect its officers not less often than once every three years by secret ballot among the members in good standing.

(c) Every national or international labor organization, except a federation of national or international labor organizations, and every local labor organization, and its officers, shall be under a duty, enforceable at the suit of any bona fide candidate for office in such labor organization in the district court of the United States in which such labor organization maintains its principal office, to comply with all reasonable requests of any candidate to distribute by mail or otherwise at the candidate's expense campaign literature in aid of such person's candidacy to all members in good standing of such labor organization and to refrain from discrimination in favor of or against any candidate with respect to the use of lists of members, and whenever such labor organizations or its officers authorize the distribution by mail or otherwise to members of campaign literature on behalf of any candidate or of the labor organization itself with reference to such election, similar distribution at the request of any other bona fide candidate shall be made by such labor organization and its officers, with equal treatment as to the expense of such distribution. Every bona fide candidate shall have the right, once within 30 days prior to an election of a labor organization in which he is a candidate, to inspect a list containing the names and last known addresses of all members of the labor organization who are subject to a collective bargaining agreement requiring membership therein as a condition of employment, which list shall be maintained and kept at the principal office of such labor organization by a designated official thereof. Adequate safeguards to insure a fair election shall be provided, including the right of any candidate to have an observer at the polls and at the counting of the ballots.

(d) Officers of intermediate bodies, such as general committees, system boards, joint boards, or joint councils, shall be elected not less often than once every four years by secret ballot among the members in good standing or by labor organization officers representative of such members who have been elected by secret ballot.

(e) In any election required by this section which is to be held by secret ballot a reasonable opportunity shall be given for the nomination of candidates and every member in good standing shall be eligible to be a candidate and to hold office (subject to section 504 and to reasonable qualifications uniformly imposed) and shall have the right to vote for or otherwise support the candidate or candidates of his choice, without being subject to penalty, discipline, or improper interference or reprisal of any kind by such organization or any member thereof. Not less than fifteen days prior to the election notice thereof shall be mailed to each member at his last known home address. Each member in good standing shall be entitled to one vote. No member whose dues have been withheld by his employer for payment to such organization pursuant to his voluntary authorization provided for in a collective bargaining agreement, shall be declared ineligible to vote or be a candidate for office in such organization by reason of alleged delay or default in the payment of dues. The votes cast by members of each local labor organization shall be counted, and the results published, separately. The election officials designated in the constitution and bylaws or the secretary, if no other official is designated, shall preserve for one year the ballots and all other records pertaining to the election. The election shall be conducted in accordance with the constitution and bylaws of such organization insofar as they are not inconsistent with the provisions of this title.

(f) When officers are chosen by a convention of delegates elected by secret ballot, the convention shall be conducted in accordance with the constitution and bylaws of the labor organization insofar as they are not inconsistent with the provisions of this title. The officials designated in the constitution and bylaws or the secretary, if no other is designated, shall preserve for one year the credentials of the delegates and all minutes and other records of the convention pertaining to the election of officers.

(g) No moneys received by any labor organization by way of dues, assessment, or similar levy, and no moneys of an employer shall be contributed or applied to promote the candidacy of any person in an election subject to the provisions of this title. Such moneys of a labor organization may be utilized for notices, factual statements of issues not involving candidates, and other expenses necessary for the holding of an election.

(h) If the Secretary, upon application of any member of a local labor organization, finds after hearing in accordance with the Administrative Procedure Act that the constitution and bylaws of such labor organization do not provide an adequate procedure for the removal of an elected officer guilty of serious misconduct, such officer may be removed, for cause shown and after notice and hearing, by the members in good standing voting in a secret ballot conducted by the officers of such labor organization in accordance with its constitution and bylaws insofar as they are not inconsistent with the provisions of this title.

(i) The Secretary shall promulgate rules and regulations prescribing minimum standards and procedures for determining the adequacy of the removal procedures to which reference is made in subsection (h).

ENFORCEMENT

Sec. 402. (a) A member of a labor organization—

(1) who has exhausted the remedies available under the constitution and bylaws of such organization and of any parent body or

(2) who has invoked such available remedies without obtaining a final decision within three calendar months after their invocation,

may file a complaint with the Secretary within one calendar month thereafter alleging the violation of any provision of section 401 (including violation of the constitution and bylaws of the labor organization pertaining to the election and removal of officers). The challenged election shall be presumed valid pending a final decision thereon (as hereinafter provided) and in the interim the affairs of the organization shall be conducted by the officers elected or in such other manner as its constitution and bylaws may provide.

(b) The Secretary shall investigate such complaint and, if he finds probable cause to believe that a violation of this title has occurred and has not been remedied, he shall, within sixty days after the filing of such complaint, bring a civil action against the labor organization as an entity in the district court of the United States in which such labor organization maintains its principal office to set aside the invalid election, if any, and to direct the conduct of an election or hearing and vote upon the removal of officers under the supervision of the Secretary and in accordance with the provisions of this title and such rules and regulations as the Secretary may prescribe. The court shall have power to take such action as it deems proper to preserve the assets of the labor organization.

(c) If, upon a preponderance of the evidence after a trial upon the merits, the court finds—

(1) that an election has not been held within the time prescribed by section 401, or

(2) that the violation of section 401 may have affected the outcome of an election

the court shall declare the election, if any, to be void and direct the conduct of a new election under supervision of the Secretary and, so far as lawful and practicable, in conformity with the constitution and bylaws of the labor organization. The Secretary shall promptly certify to the court the names of the persons elected, and the court shall thereupon enter a decree declaring such persons to be the officers of the labor organization. If the proceeding is for the removal of officers pursuant to subsection (h) of section 401, the Secretary shall certify the results of the vote and the court shall enter a decree declaring whether such persons have been removed as officers of the labor organization.

(d) An order directing an election, dismissing a complaint, or designating elected officers of a labor organization shall be appealable in the same manner as the final judgment in a civil action, but an order directing an election shall not be stayed pending appeal.

APPLICATION OF OTHER LAWS

Sec. 403. No labor organization shall be required by law to conduct elections of officers with greater frequency or in a different form or manner than is required by its own constitution or bylaws, except as otherwise provided by this title. Existing rights and remedies to enforce the constitution and bylaws of a labor organization with respect to elections prior to the conduct thereof shall not be affected by the provisions of this title. The remedy provided by this title for challenging an election already conducted shall be exclusive.

EFFECTIVE DATE

Sec. 404. The provisions of this title shall become applicable—

(1) ninety days after the date of enactment of this Act in the case of a labor organization whose constitution and bylaws can lawfully be modified or amended by action of its constitutional officers or governing body, or

(2) where such modification can only be made by a constitutional convention of the labor organization, not later than the next constitutional convention of such labor organization after the date of enactment of this Act, or one year after such date, whichever is sooner. If no such convention is held within such one-

year period, the executive board or similar governing body empowered to act for such labor organization between conventions is empowered to make such interim constitutional changes as are necessary to carry out the provisions of this title.

TITLE V—SAFEGUARDS FOR LABOR ORGANIZATIONS

FIDUCIARY RESPONSIBILITY OF OFFICERS OF LABOR ORGANIZATIONS

Sec. 501. (a) The officers, agents, shop stewards, and other representatives of a labor organization occupy positions of trust in relation to such organization and its members as a group. It is, therefore, the duty of each such person, taking into account the special problems and functions of a labor organization, to hold its money and property solely for the benefit of the organization and its members and to manage, invest, and expend the same in accordance with its constitution and bylaws and any resolutions of the governing bodies adopted thereunder, to refrain from dealing with such organization as an adverse party or in behalf of an adverse party in any matter connected with his duties and from holding or acquiring any pecuniary or personal interest which conflicts with the interests of such organization, and to account to the organization for any profit received by him in whatever capacity in connection with transactions conducted by him or under his direction on behalf of the organization. A general exculpatory provision in the constitution and bylaws of such a labor organization or a general exculpatory resolution of a governing body purporting to relieve any such person of liability for breach of the duties declared by this section shall be void as against public policy.

(b) When any officer, agent, shop steward, or representative of any labor organization is alleged to have violated the duties declared in subsection (a) and the labor organization or its governing board or officers refuse or fail to sue or recover damages or secure an accounting or other appropriate relief within a reasonable time after being requested to do so by any member of the labor organization, such member may sue such officer, agent, shop steward, or representative in any district court of the United States or in any State court of competent jurisdiction to recover damages or secure an accounting or other appropriate relief for the benefit of the labor organization. No such proceeding shall be brought except upon leave of the court obtained upon verified application and for good cause shown which application may be made ex parte. The trial judge may allot a reasonable part of the recovery in any action under this subsection to pay the fees of counsel prosecuting the suit at the instance of the member of the labor organization and to compensate such member for any expenses necessarily paid or incurred by him in connection with the litigation.

(c) Any person who embezzles, steals, or unlawfully and willfully abstracts or converts to his own use, or the use of another, any of the moneys, funds, securities, property, or other assets of a labor organization of which he is an officer, or by which he is employed, directly or indirectly, shall be fined not more than $10,000 or imprisoned for not more than five years, or both.

BONDING

Sec. 502. (a) Every officer, agent, shop steward, or other representative or employee of any labor organization (other than a labor organization whose property and annual financial receipts do not exceed $5,000 in value), or of a trust in which a labor organization is interested, who handles funds or other property thereof shall be bonded to provide protection against loss by reason of acts of fraud or dishonesty on his part directly or through connivance with others. The bond of each such person shall be fixed at the beginning of the organization's fiscal year and shall be in an amount not less than 10 per centum of the funds handled by him and his predecessor or predecessors, if any, during the preceding fiscal year, but in no case more than $500,000. If the labor organization or the trust in which a labor organization is interested does not have a preceding fiscal year, the amount of the bond shall be, in the case of a local labor organization, not less than $1,000, and in the case of any other labor organization or of a trust in which a labor organization is interested, not less than $10,000. Such bonds shall be individual or schedule in form, and shall have a corporate surety company as surety thereon. Any person who is not covered by such bonds shall not be permitted to receive, handle, disburse, or otherwise exercise custody or control of the funds or other property of a labor organization or of a trust in which a labor organization is interested. No such bond shall be placed through an agent or broker or with a surety company in which any labor organization or any officer, agent, shop steward, or other representative of a labor organization has any direct or indirect interest. Such surety company shall be a corporate surety which holds a grant of authority from the Secretary of the Treasury under the Act of July 30, 1947 (6 U.S.C. 6–13), as an acceptable surety on Federal bonds: *Provided,* That when in the opinion of the Secretary a labor organization has made other bonding arrangements which would provide the protection required by this section at comparable cost or less, he may exempt such labor organization from placing a bond through a surety company holding such grant of authority.

(b) Any person who willfully violates this section shall be fined not more than $10,000 or imprisoned for not more than one year, or both.

MAKING OF LOANS; PAYMENT OF FINES

Sec. 503. (a) No labor organization shall make directly or indirectly any loan or loans to any officer or employee of such organization which results in a total indebtedness on the part of such officer or employee to the labor organization in excess of $2,000.

(b) No labor organization or employer shall directly or indirectly pay the fine of any officer or employee convicted of any willful violation of this Act.

(c) Any person who willfully violates this section shall be fined not more than $5,000 or imprisoned for not more than one year, or both.

PROHIBITION AGAINST CERTAIN PERSONS HOLDING OFFICE

Sec. 504.* (a) No person who is or has been a member of the Communist Party or who has been convicted of, or served any part of a prison term resulting from his conviction of, robbery, bribery, extortion, embezzlement, grand larceny, burglary, arson, violation of narcotics laws, murder, rape, assault with intent to kill, assault which inflicts grievous bodily injury, or a violation of subchapter III or IV of this chapter, any felony involving abuse or misuse of such person's position or employment in a labor organization or employee benefit plan to seek or obtain an illegal gain at the expense of the members of the labor organization or the beneficiaries of the employee benefit plan, or conspiracy to commit any such crimes or attempt to commit any such crimes, or a crime in which any of the foregoing crimes is an element, shall serve or be permitted to serve—

(1) as a consultant or adviser to any labor organization,

(2) as an officer, director, trustee, member of any executive board or similar governing body, business agent, manager, organizer, employee, or representative in any capacity of any labor organization,

(3) as a labor relations consultant or adviser to a person engaged in an industry or activity affecting commerce, or as an officer, director, agent, or employee of any group or association of employers dealing with any labor organization, or in a position having specific collective bargaining authority or direct responsibility in the area of labor-management relations in any corporation or association engaged in an industry or activity affecting commerce, or

(4) in a position which entitles its occupant to a share of the proceeds of, or as an officer or executive or administrative employee of, any entity whose activities are in whole or substantial part devoted to providing goods or services to any labor organization, or

(5) in any capacity, other than in his capacity as a member of such labor organization, that involves decisionmaking authority concerning, or decisionmaking authority over, or custody of, or control of the moneys, funds, assets, or property of any labor organization,

* This section was amended by Pub.L. 98–473, Title II, § 803, Oct. 12, 1984, 98 Stat. 2133.

during or for the period of thirteen years after such conviction or after the end of such imprisonment, whichever is later, unless the sentencing court on the motion of the person convicted sets a lesser period of at least three years after such conviction or after the end of such imprisonment, whichever is later, or unless prior to the end of such period, in the case of a person so convicted or imprisoned, (A) his citizenship rights, having been revoked as a result of such conviction, have been fully restored, or (B) the United States Parole Commission determines that such person's service in any capacity referred to in clauses (1) through (5) would not be contrary to the purposes of this chapter. Prior to making any such determination the Commission shall hold an administrative hearing and shall give notice of such proceeding by certified mail to the Secretary of Labor and to State, county, and Federal prosecuting officials in the jurisdiction or jurisdictions in which such person was convicted. The Commission's determination in any such proceeding shall be final. No person shall knowingly hire, retain, employ, or otherwise place any other person to serve in any capacity in violation of this subsection.

(b) Any person who willfully violates this section shall be fined not more than $10,000 or imprisoned for not more than five years, or both.

(c) For the purpose of this section—

(1) A person shall be deemed to have been "convicted" and under the disability of "conviction" from the date of the judgment of the trial court, regardless of whether that judgment remains under appeal.

(2) A period of parole shall not be considered as part of a period of imprisonment.

(d) Whenever any person—

(1) by operation of this section, has been barred from office or other position in a labor organization as a result of a conviction, and

(2) has filed an appeal of that conviction,

any salary which would be otherwise due such person by virtue of such office or position, shall be placed in escrow by the individual employer or organization responsible for payment of such salary. Payment of such salary into escrow shall continue for the duration of the appeal or for the period of time during which such salary would be otherwise due, whichever period is shorter. Upon the final reversal of such person's conviction on appeal, the amounts in escrow shall be paid to such person. Upon the final sustaining of such person's conviction on appeal, the amounts in escrow shall be returned to the individual employer or organization responsible for payments of those amounts. Upon final reversal of such person's conviction, such person shall no longer be barred by this statute from assuming any position from which such person was previously barred.

TITLE VI—MISCELLANEOUS PROVISIONS

INVESTIGATIONS

Sec. 601. (a) The Secretary shall have power when he believes it necessary in order to determine whether any person has violated or is about to violate any provision of this Act (except title I or amendments made by this Act to other statutes) to make an investigation and in connection therewith he may enter such places and inspect such records and accounts and question such persons as he may deem necessary to enable him to determine the facts relative thereto. The Secretary may report to interested persons or officials concerning the facts required to be shown in any report required by this Act and concerning the reasons for failure or refusal to file such a report or any other matter which he deems to be appropriate as a result of such an investigation.

(b) For the purpose of any investigation provided for in this Act, the provisions of sections 9 and 10 (relating to the attendance of witnesses and the production of books, papers, and documents) of the Federal Trade Commission Act of September 16, 1914, as amended (15 U.S.C. 49, 50), are hereby made applicable to the jurisdiction, powers, and duties of the Secretary or any officers designated by him.

EXTORTIONATE PICKETING

Sec. 602. (a) It shall be unlawful to carry on picketing on or about the premises of any employer for the purpose of, or as part of any conspiracy or in furtherance of any plan or purpose for, the personal profit or enrichment of any individual (except a bona fide increase in wages or other employee benefits) by taking or obtaining any money or other thing of value from such employer against his will or with his consent.

(b) Any person who willfully violates this section shall be fined not more than $10,000 or imprisoned not more than twenty years, or both.

RETENTION OF RIGHTS UNDER OTHER FEDERAL AND STATE LAWS

Sec. 603. (a) Except as explicitly provided to the contrary, nothing in this Act shall reduce or limit the responsibilities of any labor organization or any officer, agent, shop steward, or other representative of a labor organization, or of any trust in which a labor organization is interested, under any other Federal law or under the laws of any State, and, except as explicitly provided to the contrary, nothing in this Act shall take away any right or bar any remedy to which members of a labor organization are entitled under such other Federal law or law of any State.

(b) Nothing contained in titles I, II, III, IV, V, or VI of this Act shall be construed to supersede or impair or otherwise affect the provisions of the Railway Labor Act, as amended, or any of the obligations, rights, benefits, privileges, or immunities of any carrier, employee, organization, representative, or person subject thereto; nor shall anything contained in said titles (except section 505) of this Act be construed to confer any rights, privileges, immunities, or defenses upon employers, or to impair or otherwise affect the rights of any person under the National Labor Relations Act, as amended.

EFFECT ON STATE LAWS

Sec. 604. Nothing in this Act shall be construed to impair or diminish the authority of any State to enact and enforce general criminal laws with respect to robbery, bribery, extortion, embezzlement, grand larceny, burglary, arson, violation of narcotics laws, murder, rape, assault with intent to kill, or assault which inflicts grievous bodily injury, or conspiracy to commit any of such crimes.

STATE AUTHORITY TO ENACT AND ENFORCE LEGISLATION

Sec. 604a. Notwithstanding this or any other Act regulating labor-management relations, each State shall have the authority to enact and enforce, as part of a comprehensive statutory system to eliminate the threat of pervasive racketeering activity in an industry that is, or over time has been, affected by such activity, a provision of law that applies equally to employers, employees, and collective bargaining representatives, which provision of law governs service in any position in a local labor organization which acts or seeks to act in that State as a collective bargaining representative pursuant to the National Labor Relations Act [29 U.S.C.A. § 151 et seq.], in the industry that is subject to that program.*

SERVICE OF PROCESS

Sec. 605. For the purposes of this Act, service of summons, subpoena, or other legal process of a court of the United States upon an officer or agent of a labor organization in his capacity as such shall constitute service upon the labor organization.

ADMINISTRATIVE PROCEDURE ACT

Sec. 606. The provisions of the Administrative Procedure Act shall be applicable to the issuance, amendment, or rescission of any rules or regulations, or any adjudication, authorized or required pursuant to the provisions of this Act.

OTHER AGENCIES AND DEPARTMENTS

Sec. 607. In order to avoid unnecessary expense and duplication of functions among Government agencies, the Secretary may make such arrangements or agreements for cooperation or mutual assistance in the performance of his functions under this Act and the functions of any such agency as he may find to be practicable and consistent with law. The Secretary may utilize the facilities or services of any department, agency,

---

* Pub.L. 98–473, Title II, § 2201, Oct. 12, 1984, 98 Stat. 2192.

or establishment of the United States or of any State or political subdivision of a State, including the services of any of its employees, with the lawful consent of such department, agency, or establishment; and each department, agency, or establishment of the United States is authorized and directed to cooperate with the Secretary and, to the extent permitted by law, to provide such information and facilities as he may request for his assistance in the performance of his functions under this Act. The Attorney General or his representative shall receive from the Secretary for appropriate action such evidence developed in the performance of his functions under this Act as may be found to warrant consideration for criminal prosecution under the provisions of this Act or other Federal law.

CRIMINAL CONTEMPT

Sec. 608. No person shall be punished for any criminal contempt allegedly committed outside the immediate presence of the court in connection with any civil action prosecuted by the Secretary or any other person in any court of the United States under the provisions of this Act unless the facts constituting such criminal contempt are established by the verdict of the jury in a proceeding in the district court of the United States, which jury shall be chosen and empaneled in the manner prescribed by the law governing trial juries in criminal prosecutions in the district courts of the United States.

PROHIBITION ON CERTAIN DISCIPLINE BY LABOR ORGANIZATION

Sec. 609. It shall be unlawful for any labor organization, or any officer, agent, shop steward, or other representative of a labor organization, or any employee thereof to fine, suspend, expel, or otherwise discipline any of its members for exercising any right to which he is entitled under the provisions of this Act. The provisions of section 102 shall be applicable in the enforcement of this section.

DEPRIVATION OF RIGHTS UNDER ACT BY VIOLENCE

Sec. 610. It shall be unlawful for any person through the use of force or violence, or threat of the use of force or violence, to restrain, coerce, or intimidate, or attempt to restrain, coerce, or intimidate any member of a labor organization for the purpose of interfering with or preventing the exercise of any right to which he is entitled under the provisions of this Act. Any person who willfully violates this section shall be fined not more than $1,000 or imprisoned for not more than one year, or both.

SEPARABILITY PROVISIONS

Sec. 611. If any provision of this Act, or the application of such provision to any person or circumstances, shall be held invalid, the remainder of this Act or the application of such provision to persons or circumstances other than those as to which it is held invalid, shall not be affected thereby.

Civil Rights Act of 1964

78 Stat. 253 (1964), as amended; 42 U.S.C. § 2000e et seq. (1988); as amended Pub.L. 102–166 (Nov. 21, 1991).

TITLE VII—EQUAL EMPLOYMENT OPPORTUNITY

DEFINITIONS

Sec. 701. (§ 2000e) For the purposes of this title—

(a) The term "person" includes one or more individuals, governments, governmental agencies, political subdivisions, labor unions, partnerships, associations, corporations, legal representatives, mutual companies, joint-stock companies, trusts, unincorporated organizations, trustees, trustees in bankruptcy, or receivers.

(b) The term "employer" means a person engaged in an industry affecting commerce who has fifteen or more employees for each working day in each of twenty or more calendar weeks in the current or preceding calendar year, and any agent of such a person, but such term does not include (1) the United States, a corporation wholly owned by the Government of the United States, an Indian tribe, or any department or agency of the District of Columbia subject by statute to procedures of the competitive service (as defined in section 2102 of Title 5), or (2) a bona fide private membership club (other than a labor organization) which is exempt from taxation under section 501(c) of Title 26, except that during the first year after March 24, 1972, persons having fewer than twenty-five employees (and their agents) shall not be considered employers.

(c) The term "employment agency" means any person regularly undertaking with or without compensation to procure employees for an employer or to procure for employees opportunities to work for an employer and includes an agent of such a person.

(d) The term "labor organization" means a labor organization engaged in an industry affecting commerce, and any agent of such an organization, and includes any organization of any kind, any agency, or employee representation committee, group, association, or plan so engaged in which employees participate and which exists for the purpose, in whole or in part, of dealing with employers concerning grievances, labor disputes, wages, rates of pay, hours, or other terms or conditions of employment, and any conference, general committee, joint or system board, or joint council so engaged which is subordinate to a national or international labor organization.

(e) A labor organization shall be deemed to be engaged in an industry affecting commerce if (1) it maintains or operates a hiring hall or hiring office which procures employees for an employer or procures for employees opportunities to work for an employer, or (2) the number of its members (or, where it is a labor organization composed of other labor organizations or their representatives, if the aggregate number of the members of such other labor organization) is (A) twenty-five or more during the first year after March 24, 1972, or (B) fifteen or more thereafter, and such labor organization—

(1) is the certified representative of employees under the provisions of the National Labor Relations Act, as amended, or the Railway Labor Act, as amended;

(2) although not certified, is a national or international labor organization or a local labor organization recognized or acting as the representative of employees of an employer or employers engaged in an industry affecting commerce; or

(3) has chartered a local labor organization or subsidiary body which is representing or actively seeking to represent employees of employers within the meaning of paragraph (1) or (2); or

(4) has been chartered by a labor organization representing or actively seeking to represent employees within the meaning of paragraph (1) or (2) as the local or subordinate body through which such employees may enjoy membership or become affiliated with such labor organization; or

(5) is a conference, general committee, joint or system board, or joint council subordinate to a national or international labor organization, which includes a labor organization engaged in an industry affecting commerce within the meaning of any of the preceding paragraphs of this subsection.

(f) The term "employee" means an individual employed by an employer, except that the term "employee" shall not include any person elected to public office in any State or political subdivision of any State by the qualified voters thereof, or any person chosen by such officer to be on such officer's personal staff, or an appointee on the policy making level or an immediate adviser with respect to the exercise of the constitutional or legal powers of the office. The exemption set forth in the preceding sentence shall not include employees subject to the civil service laws of a State government, governmental agency or political subdivision. With respect to employment in a foreign country, such term includes an individual who is a citizen of the United States.

(g) The term "commerce" means trade, traffic, commerce, transportation, transmission, or communication among the several States; or between a State and any place outside thereof; or within the District of Columbia, or a possession of the United States; or between points in the same State but through a point outside thereof.

(h) The term "industry affecting commerce" means any activity, business, or industry in commerce or in which a labor dispute would hinder or obstruct commerce or the free flow of commerce and includes any activity or industry "affecting commerce" within the meaning of the Labor-Management Reporting and Disclosure Act of 1959, and further includes any governmental industry, business, or activity.

(i) The term "State" includes a State of the United States, the District of Columbia, Puerto Rico, the Virgin Islands, American Samoa, Guam, Wake Island, the Canal Zone, and Outer Continental Shelf lands defined in the Outer Continental Shelf Lands Act.

(j) The term "religion" includes all aspects of religious observance and practice, as well as belief, unless an employer demonstrates that he is unable to reasonably accommodate to an employee's or prospective employee's religious observance or practice without undue hardship on the conduct of the employer's business.

(k) The terms "because of sex" or "on the basis of sex" include, but are not limited to, because of or on the basis of pregnancy, childbirth, or related medical conditions; and women affected by pregnancy, childbirth, or related medical conditions shall be treated the same for all employment-related purposes, including receipt of benefits under fringe benefit programs, as other persons not so affected but similar in their ability or inability to work, and nothing in section 2(h) of this Act shall be interpreted to permit otherwise. This subsection shall not require an employer to pay for health insurance benefits for abortion, except where the life of the mother would be endangered if the fetus were carried to term, or except where medical complications have arisen from an abortion: *Provided*, That nothing herein shall preclude an employer from providing abortion benefits or otherwise affect bargaining agreements in regard to abortion.

(*l*) The term "complaining party" means the Commission, the Attorney General, or a person who may bring an action or proceeding under this subchapter.

(m) The term "demonstrates" means meets the burdens of production and persuasion.

(n) The term "respondent" means an employer, employment agency, labor organization, joint labor-management committee controlling apprenticeship or other training or retraining program, including an on-the-job training program, or Federal entity subject to section 2000e–16 of this title.

FOREIGN AND RELIGIOUS EMPLOYMENT

Sec. 702. (§ 2000e–1)(a) This Subchapter shall not apply to an employer with respect to the employment of aliens outside any State, or to a religious corporation, association, educational institution, or society with respect to the employment of individuals of a particular religion to perform work connected with the carrying on by such corporation, association, educational institution, or society of its activities.

(b) It shall not be unlawful under section 2000e–2 or 2000e–3 of this title for an employer (or a corporation controlled by an employer), labor organization, employment agency, or joint labor-management committee controlling apprenticeship or other training or retraining (including on-the-job training programs) to take any action otherwise prohibited by such section, with respect to an employee in a workplace in a foreign country if compliance with such section would cause such employer (or such corporation), such organization, such agency, or such committee to violate the law of the foreign country in which such workplace is located.

(c)(1) If an employer controls a corporation whose place of incorporation is a foreign country, any practice prohibited by section 2000e–2 or 2000e–3 of this title engaged in by such corporation shall be presumed to be engaged in by such employer.

(2) Sections 2000e–2 and 2000e–3 of this title shall not apply with respect to the foreign operations of an employer that is a foreign person not controlled by an American employer.

(3) For purposes of this subsection, the determination of whether an employer controls a corporation shall be based on—

(A) the interrelation of operations;

(B) the common management;

(C) the centralized control of labor relations; and

(D) the common ownership or financial control,

of the employer and the corporation.

DISCRIMINATION BECAUSE OF RACE, COLOR, RELIGION, SEX, OR NATIONAL ORIGIN

Sec. 703. (§ 2000e–2)(a) It shall be an unlawful employment practice for an employer—

(1) to fail or refuse to hire or to discharge any individual, or otherwise to discriminate against any individual with respect to his compensation, terms, conditions, or privileges of employment, because of such individual's race, color, religion, sex, or national origin; or

(2) to limit, segregate, or classify his employees or applicants for employment in any way which would deprive or tend to deprive any individual of employment opportunities or otherwise adversely affect his status as an employee, because of such individual's race, color, religion, sex, or national origin.

(b) It shall be an unlawful employment practice for an employment agency to fail or refuse to refer for employment, or otherwise to discriminate against, any individual because of his race, color, religion, sex, or national origin, or to classify or refer for employment any individual on the basis of his race, color, religion, sex, or national origin.

(c) It shall be an unlawful employment practice for a labor organization—

(1) to exclude or to expel from its membership, or otherwise to discriminate against, any individual because of his race, color, religion, sex, or national origin;

(2) to limit, segregate, or classify its membership or applicants for membership, or to classify or fail or refuse to refer for employment any individual, in any way which would deprive or tend to deprive any individual of employment opportunities, or would limit such employment opportunities or otherwise adversely affect his status as an employee or as an applicant for employment, because of such individual's race, color, religion, sex, or national origin; or

(3) to cause or attempt to cause an employer to discriminate against an individual in violation of this section.

(d) It shall be an unlawful employment practice for any employer, labor organization, or joint labor-management committee controlling apprenticeship or other training or retraining, including on-the-job training programs to discriminate against any individual because of his race, color, religion, sex, or national origin in admission to, or employment in, any program established to provide apprenticeship or other training.

(e) Notwithstanding any other provision of this Subchapter (1) it shall not be an unlawful employment practice for an employer to hire and employ employees, for an employment agency to classify, or refer for employment any individual, for a labor organization to classify its membership or to classify or refer for employment any individual, or for an employer, labor organization, or joint labor-management committee controlling apprenticeship or other training or retraining programs to admit or employ any individual in any such program, on the basis of his religion, sex, or national origin in those certain instances where religion, sex, or national origin is a bona fide occupational qualification reasonably necessary to the normal operation of that particular business or enterprise, and (2) it shall not be an unlawful employment practice for a school, college, university, or other educational institution or institution of learning to hire and employ employees of a particular religion if such school, college, university, or other educational institution or institution of learning is, in whole or in substantial part, owned, supported, controlled, or managed by a particular religion or by a particular religious corporation, association, or society, or if the curriculum of such school, college, university, or other educational institution or institution of learning is directed toward the propagation of a particular religion.

(f) As used in this Subchapter, the phrase "unlawful employment practice" shall not be deemed to include any action or measure taken by an employer, labor organization, joint labor-management committee, or employment agency with respect to an individual who is a member of the Communist Party of the United States or of any other organization required to register as a Communist-action or Communist-front organization by final order of the Subversive Activities Control Board pursuant to the Subversive Activities Control Act of 1950.

(g) Notwithstanding any other provision of this Subchapter, it shall not be an unlawful employment practice for an employer to fail or refuse to hire and employ any individual for any position, for an employer to discharge any individual from any position, or for an employment agency to fail or refuse to refer any individual for employment in any position, or for a labor organization to fail or refuse to refer any individual for employment in any position, if—

(1) the occupancy of such position, or access to the premises in or upon which any part of the duties of such position is performed or is to be performed, is subject to any requirement imposed in the interest of the national security of the United States under any security program in effect pursuant to or administered under any statute of the United States or any Executive order of the President; and

(2) such individual has not fulfilled or has ceased to fulfill that requirement.

(h) Notwithstanding any other provision of this Subchapter, it shall not be an unlawful employment practice for an employer to apply different standards of compensation, or different terms, conditions, or privileges of employment pursuant to a bona fide seniority or merit system, or a system which measures earnings by quantity or quality of production or to employees who work in different locations, provided that such differences are not the result of an intention to discriminate because of race, color, religion, sex, or national origin, nor shall it be an unlawful employment practice for an employer to give and to act upon the results of any professionally developed ability test provided that such test, its administration or action upon the results is not designed, intended or used to discriminate because of race, color, religion, sex or national origin. It shall not be an unlawful employment practice under this subchapter for any employer to differentiate upon the basis of sex in determining the amount of the wages or compensation paid or to be paid to employees of such employer if such differentiation is authorized by the provisions of section 206(d) of Title 29.

(i) Nothing contained in this Subchapter shall apply to any business or enterprise on or near an Indian reservation with respect to any publicly announced employment practice of such business or enterprise under which a preferential treatment is given to any individual because he is an Indian living on or near a reservation.

(j) Nothing contained in this Subchapter shall be interpreted to require any employer, employment agency, labor organization, or joint labor-management committee subject to this subchapter to grant preferential treatment to any individual or to any group because of the race, color, religion, sex, or national origin of such individual or group on account of an imbalance which may exist with respect to the total number of percentage of persons of any race, color, religion, sex, or national origin employed by any employer, referred or classified for employment by any employment agency or labor organization, admitted to membership or classified by any labor organization, or admitted to, or employed in, any apprenticeship or other training program, in comparison with the total number or percentage of persons of such race, color, religion, sex, or national origin in any community, State, section, or other area, or in the available work force in any community, State, section, or other area.

(k)(1)**(A)** An unlawful employment practice based on disparate impact is established under this subchapter only if—

(i) a complaining party demonstrates that a respondent uses a particular employment practice that causes a disparate impact on the basis of race, color, religion, sex, or national origin and the respondent fails to demonstrate that the challenged practice is job related for the position in question and consistent with business necessity; or

(ii) the complaining party makes the demonstration described in subparagraph (C) with respect to an alternative employment practice and the respondent refuses to adopt such alternative employment practice.

(B)(i) With respect to demonstrating that a particular employment practice causes a disparate impact as described in subparagraph (A)(i), the complaining party shall demonstrate that each particular challenged employment practice causes a disparate impact, except that if the complaining party can demonstrate to the court that the elements of a respondent's decisionmaking process are not capable of separation for analysis, the decisionmaking process may be analyzed as one employment practice.

(ii) If the respondent demonstrates that a specific employment practice does not cause the disparate impact, the respondent shall not be required to demonstrate that such practice is required by business necessity.

(C) The demonstration referred to by subparagraph (A)(ii) shall be in accordance with the law as it existed on June 4, 1989, with respect to the concept of "alternative employment practice".

(2) A demonstration that an employment practice is required by business necessity may not be used as a defense against a claim of intentional discrimination under this subchapter.

(3) Notwithstanding any other provision of this subchapter, a rule barring the employment of an individual who currently and knowingly uses or possesses a controlled substance, as defined in schedules I and II of section 102(6) of the Controlled Substances Act (21 U.S.C. 802(6)), other than the use or possession of a drug taken under the supervision of a licensed health care professional, or any other use or possession authorized by the Controlled Substances Act or any other provision of Federal law, shall be considered an unlawful employment practice under this subchapter only if such

rule is adopted or applied with an intent to discriminate because of race, color, religion, sex, or national origin.

(*l*) It shall be an unlawful employment practice for a respondent, in connection with the selection or referral of applicants or candidates for employment or promotion, to adjust the scores of, use different cutoff scores for, or otherwise alter the results of, employment related tests on the basis of race, color, religion, sex, or national origin.

(m) Except as otherwise provided in this subchapter, an unlawful employment practice is established when the complaining party demonstrates that race, color, religion, sex, or national origin was a motivating factor for any employment practice, even though other factors also motivated the practice.

(n)(1)**(A)** Notwithstanding any other provision of law, and except as provided in paragraph (2), an employment practice that implements and is within the scope of a litigated or consent judgment or order that resolves a claim of employment discrimination under the Constitution or Federal civil rights laws may not be challenged under the circumstances described in subparagraph (B).

(B) A practice described in subparagraph (A) may not be challenged in a claim under the Constitution or Federal civil rights laws—

(i) by a person who, prior to the entry of the judgment or order described in subparagraph (A), had—

(I) actual notice of the proposed judgment or order sufficient to apprise such person that such judgment or order might adversely affect the interests and legal rights of such person and that an opportunity was available to present objections to such judgment or order by a future date certain; and

(II) a reasonable opportunity to present objections to such judgment or order; or

(ii) by a person whose interests were adequately represented by another person who had previously challenged the judgment or order on the same legal grounds and with a similar factual situation, unless there has been an intervening change in law or fact.

(2) Nothing in this subsection shall be construed to—

(A) alter the standards for intervention under rule 24 of the Federal Rules of Civil Procedure or apply to the rights of parties who have successfully intervened pursuant to such rule in the proceeding in which the parties intervened;

(B) apply to the rights of parties to the action in which a litigated or consent judgment or order was entered, or of members of a class represented or sought to be represented in such action, or of members of a group on whose behalf relief was sought in such action by the Federal Government;

(C) prevent challenges to a litigated or consent judgment or order on the ground that such judgment or order was obtained through collusion or fraud, or is transparently invalid or was entered by a court lacking subject matter jurisdiction; or

(D) authorize or permit the denial to any person of the due process of law required by the Constitution.

(3) Any action not precluded under this subsection that challenges an employment consent judgment or order described in paragraph (1) shall be brought in the court, and if possible before the judge, that entered such judgment or order. Nothing in this subsection shall preclude a transfer of such action pursuant to section 1404 of Title 28.

OTHER UNLAWFUL EMPLOYMENT PRACTICES

Sec. 704. (§ 2000e–3)(a) It shall be an unlawful employment practice for an employer to discriminate against any of his employees or applicants for employment, for an employment agency, or joint labor-management committee controlling apprenticeship or other training or retraining, including on-the-job training programs, to discriminate against any individual, or for a labor organization to discriminate against any member thereof or applicant for membership, because he has opposed any practice made an unlawful employment practice by this subchapter, or because he has made a charge, testified, assisted, or participated in any manner in an investigation, proceeding, or hearing under this subchapter.

(b) It shall be an unlawful employment practice for an employer, labor organization, employment agency, or joint labor-management committee controlling apprenticeship or other training or retraining; including on-the-job training programs, to print or publish or cause to be printed or published any notice or advertisement relating to employment by such an employer or membership in or any classification or referral for employment by such a labor organization, or relating to any classification or referral for employment by such an employment agency, or relating to admission to, or employment in, any program established to provide apprenticeship or other training by such a joint labor management committee, indicating any preference, limitation, specification, or discrimination, based on race, color, religion, sex, or national origin, except that such a notice or advertisement may indicate a preference, limitation, specification, or discrimination based on religion, sex, or national origin when religion, sex, or national origin is a bona fide occupational qualification for employment.

* * *

WORKER ADJUSTMENT AND RETRAINING NOTIFICATION ACT

102 Stat. 890 (1988), 29 U.S.C. §§ 2101–2109 (1988).

§ 2101. Definitions; exclusions from definition of loss of employment

(a) Definitions.—As used in this chapter—

(1) the term "employer" means any business enterprise that employs—

(A) 100 or more employees, excluding part-time employees; or

(B) 100 or more employees who in the aggregate work at least 4,000 hours per week (exclusive of hours of overtime);

(2) the term "plant closing" means the permanent or temporary shutdown of a single site of employment, or one or more facilities or operating units within a single site of employment, if the shutdown results in an employment loss at the single site of employment during any 30-day period for 50 or more employees excluding any part-time employees;

(3) the term "mass layoff" means a reduction in force which—

(A) is not the result of a plant closing; and

(B) results in an employment loss at the single site of employment during any 30-day period for—

(i)(I) at least 33 percent of the employees (excluding any part-time employees); and

(II) at least 50 employees (excluding any part-time employees); or

(ii) at least 500 employees (excluding any part-time employees);

(4) the term "representative" means an exclusive representative of employees within the meaning of section 158(f) or 159(a) of this title or section 152 of Title 45;

(5) the term "affected employees" means employees who may reasonably be expected to experience an employment loss as a consequence of a proposed plant closing or mass layoff by their employer;

(6) subject to subsection (b) of this section the term "employment loss" means (A) an employment termination, other than a discharge for cause, voluntary departure, or retirement, (B) a layoff exceeding 6 months, or (C) a reduction in hours of work of more than 50 percent during each month of any 6-month period;

(7) the term "unit of local government" means any general purpose political subdivision of a State which has the power to levy taxes and spend funds, as well as general corporate and police powers; and

(8) the term "part-time employee" means an employee who is employed for an average of fewer than 20 hours per week or who has been employed for fewer than 6 of the 12 months preceding the date on which notice is required.

(b) Exclusions from definition of employment loss.—(1) In the case of a sale of part or all of an employer's business, the seller shall be responsible for providing notice for any plant closing or mass layoff in accordance with section 2102 of this title, up to and including the effective date of the sale. After the effective date of the sale of part or all of an employer's business, the purchaser shall be responsible for providing notice for any plant closing or mass layoff in accordance with section 2102 of this title. Notwithstanding any other provision of this chapter, any person who is an employee of the seller (other than a part-time employee) as of the effective date of the sale shall be considered an employee of the purchaser immediately after the effective date of the sale.

(2) Notwithstanding subsection (a)(6) of this section, an employee may not be considered to have experienced an employment loss if the closing or layoff is the result of the relocation or consolidation of part or all of the employer's business and, prior to the closing or layoff—

(A) the employer offers to transfer the employee to a different site of employment within a reasonable commuting distance with no more than a 6-month break in employment; or

(B) the employer offers to transfer the employee to any other site of employment regardless of distance with no more than a 6-month break in employment, and the employee accepts within 30 days of the offer or of the closing or layoff, whichever is later.

§ 2102. Notice required before plant closings and mass layoffs

(a) Notice to employees, state dislocated worker units, and local governments.—An employer shall not order a plant closing or mass layoff until the end of a 60-day period after the employer serves written notice of such an order—

(1) to each representative of the affected employees as of the time of the notice or, if there is no such representative at that time, to each affected employee; and

(2) to the State dislocated worker unit (designated or created under title III of the Job Training Partnership Act [29 U.S.C.A.

§ 1651 et seq.]), and the chief elected official of the unit of local government within which such closing or layoff is to occur.

If there is more than one such unit, the unit of local government which the employer shall notify is the unit of local government to which the employer pays the highest taxes for the year preceding the year for which the determination is made.

(b) Reduction of notification period.—(1) An employer may order the shutdown of a single site of employment before the conclusion of the 60-day period if as of the time that notice would have been required the employer was actively seeking capital or business which, if obtained, would have enabled the employer to avoid or postpone the shutdown and the employer reasonably and in good faith believed that giving the notice required would have precluded the employer from obtaining the needed capital or business.

(2)(A) An employer may order a plant closing or mass layoff before the conclusion of the 60-day period if the closing or mass layoff is caused by business circumstances that were not reasonably foreseeable as of the time that notice would have been required.

(B) No notice under this chapter shall be required if the plant closing or mass layoff is due to any form of natural disaster, such as a flood, earthquake, or the drought currently ravaging the farmlands of the United States.

(3) An employer relying on this subsection shall give as much notice as is practicable and at that time shall give a brief statement of the basis for reducing the notification period.

(c) Extension of layoff period.—A layoff of more than 6 months which, at its outset, was announced to be a layoff of 6 months or less, shall be treated as an employment loss under this chapter unless—

(1) the extension beyond 6 months is caused by business circumstances (including unforeseeable changes in price or cost) not reasonably foreseeable at the time of the initial layoff; and

(2) notice is given at the time it becomes reasonably foreseeable, that the extension beyond 6 months will be required.

(d) Determinations with respect to employment loss.—For purposes of this section, in determining whether a plant closing or mass layoff has occurred or will occur, employment losses for 2 or more groups at a single site of employment, each of which is less than the minimum number of employees specified in section 2101(a)(2) or (3) of this title but which in the aggregate exceed that minimum number, and which occur within any 90-day period shall be considered to be a plant closing or mass layoff unless the employer demonstrates that the employment losses are the result of separate and distinct actions and causes and are not an attempt by the employer to evade the requirements of this chapter.

§ 2103. Exemptions

This chapter shall not apply to a plant closing or mass layoff if—

(1) the closing is of a temporary facility or the closing or layoff is the result of the completion of a particular project or undertaking, and the affected employees were hired with the understanding that their employment was limited to the duration of the facility or the project or undertaking; or

(2) the closing or layoff constitutes a strike or constitutes a lockout not intended to evade the requirements of this chapter. Nothing in this chapter shall require an employer to serve written notice pursuant to section 2102(a) of this title when permanently replacing a person who is deemed to be an economic striker under the National Labor Relations Act [29 U.S.C.A. § 151 et seq.]: *Provided,* That nothing in this chapter shall be deemed to validate or invalidate any judicial or administrative ruling relating to the hiring of permanent replacements for economic strikers under the National Labor Relations Act.

§ 2104. Administration and enforcement of requirements

(a) Civil actions against employers.—(1) Any employer who orders a plant closing or mass layoff in violation of section 2102 of this title shall be liable to each aggrieved employee who suffers an employment loss as a result of such closing or layoff for—

(A) back pay for each day of violation at a rate of compensation not less than the higher of—

(i) the average regular rate received by such employee during the last 3 years of the employee's employment; or

(ii) the final regular rate received by such employee; and

(B) benefits under an employee benefit plan described in section 1002(3) of this title, including the cost of medical expenses incurred during the employment loss which would have been covered under an employee benefit plan if the employment loss had not occurred.

Such liability shall be calculated for the period of the violation, up to a maximum of 60 days, but in no event for more than one-half the number of days the employee was employed by the employer.

(2) The amount for which an employer is liable under paragraph (1) shall be reduced by—

(A) any wages paid by the employer to the employee for the period of the violation;

(B) any voluntary and unconditional payment by the employer to the employee that is not required by any legal obligation; and

(C) any payment by the employer to a third party or trustee (such as premiums for health benefits or payments to a defined contribution pension plan) on behalf of and attributable to the employee for the period of the violation.

In addition, any liability incurred under paragraph (1) with respect to a defined benefit pension plan may be reduced by crediting the employee with service for all purposes under such a plan for the period of the violation.

(3) Any employer who violates the provisions of section 2102 of this title with respect to a unit of local government shall be subject to a civil penalty of not more than $500 for each day of such violation, except that such penalty shall not apply if the employer pays to each aggrieved employee the amount for which the employer is liable to that employee within 3 weeks from the date the employer orders the shutdown or layoff.

(4) If an employer which has violated this chapter proves to the satisfaction of the court that the act or omission that violated this chapter was in good faith and that the employer had reasonable grounds for believing that the act or omission was not a violation of this chapter the court may, in its discretion, reduce the amount of the liability or penalty provided for in this section.

(5) A person seeking to enforce such liability, including a representative of employees or a unit of local government aggrieved under paragraph (1) or (3), may sue either for such person or for other persons similarly situated, or both, in any district court of the United States for any district in which the violation is alleged to have occurred, or in which the employer transacts business.

(6) In any such suit, the court, in its discretion, may allow the prevailing party a reasonable attorney's fee as part of the costs.

(7) For purposes of this subsection, the term, "aggrieved employee" means an employee who has worked for the employer ordering the plant closing or mass layoff and who, as a result of the failure by the employer to comply with section 2102 of this title, did not receive timely notice either directly or through his or her representative as required by section 2102 of this title.

(b) Exclusivity of remedies.—The remedies provided for in this section shall be the exclusive remedies for any violation of this chapter. Under this chapter, a Federal court shall not have authority to enjoin a plant closing or mass layoff.

§ 2105. Procedures in addition to other rights of employees

The rights and remedies provided to employees by this chapter are in addition to, and not in lieu of, any other contractual or statutory rights and remedies of the employees, and are not intended to alter or affect such rights and remedies, except that the period of notification required by this chapter shall run concurrently with any period of notification required by contract or by any other statute.

§ 2106. Procedures encouraged where not required

It is the sense of Congress that an employer who is not required to comply with the notice requirements of section 2102 of this title should, to the extent possible, provide notice to its employees about a proposal to close a plant or permanently reduce its workforce.

§ 2107. Authority to prescribe regulations

(a) The Secretary of Labor shall prescribe such regulations as may be necessary to carry out this chapter. Such regulations shall, at a minimum, include interpretative regulations describing the methods by which employers may provide for appropriate service of notice as required by this chapter.

(b) The mailing of notice to an employee's last known address or inclusion of notice in the employee's paycheck will be considered acceptable methods for fulfillment of the employer's obligation to give notice to each affected employee under this chapter.

§ 2108. Effect on other laws

The giving of notice pursuant to this chapter, if done in good faith compliance with this chapter, shall not constitute a violation of the National Labor Relations Act [29 U.S.C.A. § 151 et seq.] or the Railway Labor Act [45 U.S.C.A. 151 et seq.].

§ 2109. Report on employment and international competitiveness

Two years after Aug. 4, 1988, the Comptroller General shall submit to the Committee on Small Business of both the House and Senate, the Committee on Labor and Human Resources, and the Committee on Education and Labor a report containing a detailed and objective analysis of the effect of this chapter on employers (especially small- and medium-sized businesses), the economy (international competitiveness), and employees (in terms of levels and conditions of employment). The Comptroller General shall assess both costs and benefits, including the effect on productivity, competitiveness, unemployment rates and compensation, and worker retraining and readjustment.

Collective Bargaining Agreement

PREAMBLE

This Agreement is made and entered into by and between the MAJOR CONTAINER COMPANY ("Company"), their successors or assigns, and the UNITED PAPERWORKERS INTERNATIONAL UNION, AFL-CIO ("Union").

I. PURPOSE

Section 1. WITNESSETH, whereas the parties hereto have reached agreement as a result of collective bargaining for the purpose of facilitating the peaceful adjustment of differences which may arise from time to time between this Company and the Union, and to promote harmony and efficiency and to the end that the employees and the Company and the general public may mutually benefit, the parties hereto contract and agree with each other as follows:

II. RECOGNITION AND UNION SECURITY

Section 1. The Company recognizes the Union as the sole agency for collective bargaining on behalf of all employees, with the exception of timekeepers, clerks, office employees, watchmen and non-working foremen and non-working supervisors, in charge of any classes of labor.

Section 2. This recognition is interpreted by the parties to apply to any transfer or relocation of the Company's present facility to another location within or outside of the metropolitan area, which are an accretion to the existing bargaining unit, where the jobs performed are substantially the same as are covered by the present Agreement.

Section 3. All employees with the exceptions noted in Section 1 who are members of the Union in good standing on the effective date of this Agreement, shall as a condition of continued employment, maintain their membership in good standing in the Union. All employees, who on the effective date of this Agreement, are not as yet members in good standing of the Union, shall become members of the Union in good standing by no later than thirty (30) days following the effective date of this Agreement and shall maintain membership in good standing in the Union in order to continue in employment. All new employees, shall as a condition of continued employment, become members and maintain membership in good standing in the Union by no later than thirty (30) days following the date of their employment or the effective date of this Agreement, whichever is the later.

Section 4. The Company agrees to discharge any employee who does not join or maintain his membership in good standing in the Union within seven (7) calendar days after receipt of written notice from the Union that such employee is delinquent in initiation fee or dues. The Union will indemnify and save harmless the Company against any and all claims, demands, or suits that may arise out of the discharge of any employee under this section.

Section 5. During the term of this Agreement, and at the written request of the Union, the Company will deduct from their wages and remit promptly to the Union the regular monthly membership dues and/or initiation fees established by the Union in accordance with the Constitution and By-Laws of the Union for all employees who have executed and caused to be delivered to the Company a written authorization for such deductions, on a form in conformity with the applicable statutes, which shall not be irrevocable for a period of more than one (1) year, or the termination date of this Agreement, whichever occurs sooner.

III. MANAGEMENT RIGHTS

Section 1. It is understood and agreed that the management of the Plant and the direction of the work force, including but not limited to the right to hire, suspend, transfer or discharge for proper cause and the right to relieve employees from duty because of lack of work, the right to establish, determine, and maintain reasonable standards of production, to introduce new and improved methods, materials, equipment or facilities and change or eliminate methods, materials, equipment or facilities are vested exclusively in the Company, subject to the provisions of this Agreement.

IV. DISCRIMINATION

Section 1. No employee shall be discriminated against by the Company for activity in or on behalf of the Union, but shall not be exempted from discipline that is not discriminatory.

Section 2. The Company and the Union agree that there shall be no discrimination in regard to hiring, tenure of employment or any condition of employment, or in regard to membership in the Union, because of race, color, religion, sex, age, disability, national origin, marital status, sexual orientation, veteran status, or any other classification protected by law.

Section 3. The parties recognize that in complying with this Article they are subject to the specific provisions and exemptions of Title VII of the Civil Rights Act of 1964, the Age Discrimination in Employment Act of 1967, the Americans with Disabilities Act, as well as the specific statutes of the various states and pertinent Executive Orders issued by the President of the United States.

V. WAGES

Section 1. The schedule of rates attached hereto as "Exhibit A" shall become a part of this Agreement and they shall be the minimum rates of pay to be paid by the Company to its employees for the duration of this Agreement.

Section 2. All employees shall receive their pay weekly.

VI. HOURS OF WORK; OVERTIME

Section 1. Eight (8) consecutive hours, shall constitute a normal day's work; five (5) days, shall constitute a normal work week. Employees assigned to work days will be granted an unpaid lunch period of thirty (30) minutes. Shift employees will be granted a paid twenty (20) minutes lunch period during the shift, when operating requirements permit. Any employee who works over eight (8) hours in any twenty-four (24) hour period, or forty (40) hours (for which overtime has not previously been paid) in any one work week, shall be paid at the rate of time and a half. This provision shall not be construed to guarantee any specific hours or days of work.

Any employee who works over sixty (60) hours (for which double-time has not previously been paid) in any one work week shall be paid at the rate of double-time.

Section 2. Overtime shall be distributed as equitably as possible among the employees who can perform the work. The Company shall maintain open overtime records for the purpose of distributing over time equitably.

Section 3. All work performed on Sundays and holidays shall be paid for at the rate of double time.

Section 4. All work performed on Saturdays shall be paid for at the rate of time and one-half.

Section 5. Employees working on second shift shall receive a shift premium of fifteen (15) cents per hour.

Section 6. Employees working on third shift shall receive a shift premium of twenty-five (25) cents per hour.

VII. HOLIDAYS

Section 1. The following holidays or days celebrated in place thereof shall be observed and shall be paid for even though not worked at eight hours of the regular hourly rate of pay for all employees who have worked sixty (60) days or more in the Company. Holidays falling on Sunday shall be observed on the following Monday.

New Year's Day

Decoration Day

Fourth of July

Good Friday

Labor Day

Employee's Birthday

Thanksgiving Day

Day after Thanksgiving

Christmas Day

Christmas Eve Day

New Year's Eve Day

Section 2. Any employee entitled to a holiday with pay shall not be required to work on said holiday.

Section 3. It is agreed that to qualify for such holiday pay an employee shall have worked the regular scheduled work day immediately preceding and succeeding said holiday, provided work is available unless excused from such work by the plant management.

VIII. VACATIONS

Section 1. Vacation pay shall be computed on the basis of regular hourly rates of pay.

Section 2. The following schedule shall be the method of application of vacation periods and vacation pay.

Length of Service	Vacation Periods	Vacation Pay at Regular Hourly Rates of Pay
1 Year	1	42 Hours Pay
3 Years	2	84 Hours Pay
8 Years	3	126 Hours Pay
15 Years	4	168 Hours Pay
20 Years	5	210 Hours Pay
25 Years	6	252 Hours Pay

Section 3. The Company may shut down the plant completely or partially to grant vacations to all or part of the employees at one time provided it shall notify the employees of such a plan at least sixty (60) days before a vacation commences. Otherwise, vacations will be scheduled according to employees' desires, subject to the exclusive right of the Company to change vacation periods to assure orderly and efficient operation of the Plant. In the event of a dispute between two or more employees as to the time of their vacations, the employee with the greatest seniority with the Company shall receive the preference.

Section 4. Any employee eligible for a vacation, who is severed from the payroll of the Company in any calendar year before having taken his or her vacation, except one who is discharged for cause or who quits without two weeks' notice, shall receive vacation pay.

IX. SENIORITY

Section 1. Seniority is defined as the length of an employee's service with the Company within the bargaining unit; it shall apply plant-wide.

Section 2. The Company agrees to draw up a plant-wide Seniority list as of June 1st of each year, which shall be posted in a location available to all employees.

Section 3. The Union may select from the employees covered by this Agreement a Steward who has been employed by the Company for a period of at least one (1) year, whose duty it is to see that this contract is not broken by either the employees or the Employer. The Union shall notify the Company, in writing, of the name of the Shop Steward.

Section 4. In the event of layoff, all Union officers, shop stewards, and shop committee members shall have seniority during their terms of office only, over other employees of the Company provided they have at least one (1) year service with the Company.

Section 5. Production foremen, or other non-bargaining unit employees, shall not do any work, the performance of which, would cause any employee to suffer lay-off or loss of overtime.

Section 6. An employee shall be terminated and shall lose all accumulated seniority when he or she:

a) quits

b) is discharged

c) is laid off for lack of work for a continuous period of 15 calendar months or a period of time equal to the employee's plant seniority, whichever comes first

d) fails to return to work within four (4) days of notice to return to work, unless such failure to return is for reason satisfactory to the Company

e) engages in gainful employment during a leave of absence except in cases where such leave of absence is expressly granted for this purpose

f) fails to return to work within three (3) working days from the date of expiration of his leave of absence

g) is absent due to non-industrial accident or illness for a period of two (2) years

h) is retired under the Company's Pension Plan.

X. PERMANENT VACANCIES

Section 1. Each permanent job vacancy and each permanent new job which falls within the scope of the Union's certification shall be filled as follows:

(a) Notice of such job shall be posted in the plant for two (2) days. Such job postings shall include the job classification, department, and the shift on which the new job or vacancy exists. Any employee who wishes to bid for such jobs shall sign the posting. Job postings shall be placed in three locations throughout the plant for official signing in the presence of a member of management, who will initial the posting. Two postings will be provided in the supervisory offices assigned in the plant; a third posting will be placed in the Human Resources office for signing. At all posting locations, job descriptions for all jobs will be available for review. At the end of the two (2) days, the Company shall remove the posting.

(b) Where skill and ability are relatively equal, seniority shall prevail, providing the employee is physically able to perform the work without endangering his or her health or safety. The most senior qualified employee will be awarded the job and be notified by the Human Resources office within five (5) days after removal of the posting. The Company will transfer the employee awarded the vacancy hereunder to the new job within fifteen (15) calendar days, provided the release of the employee does not interfere with the efficient operations of the department. Multiple postings will be awarded from the highest pay grade posting to the lowest pay grade posting.

(c) An employee awarded the vacancy hereunder shall be given up to sixteen (16) working days in which to demonstrate his or her ability to perform the work involved. In some circumstances, extensions may be required, not to exceed sixteen (16) additional workdays. During the qualifying period, employees are unable to bid. During this period, the Company may remove the employee from the job if the Company considers the employee's work to be unsatisfactory. The employee may then bid on any other vacancy. An employee disqualified from a job will be unable to bid that job for a period of three (3) months.

Section 2. The Union and the Company may, by mutual agreement, provide rules whereby disabled employees may be assigned to jobs which they are able to satisfactorily perform without regard to this Article. When the Union and the Company agree to placement of an employee hereunder, the conditions pertaining to that placement shall be reduced to writing and signed by the parties.

XI. LAYOFF AND RECALL

Section 1. If the Company decides to reduce the number of employees in a job classification in a department, and the reduction is expected to continue for more than four (4) days, the reduction shall be made as follows:

(a) The least senior employee or employees shall be removed from the classification provided the skill and ability of the employees in the classification are relatively equal.

(b) An employee removed from his or her classification and/or shift pursuant to (a) shall be afforded the opportunity to move into a job classification in an equal or lower labor grade on any shift provided he or she has the proven skill and ability to perform such work which is held by an employee with less seniority. An employee displaced from his job classification by the exercise of the seniority rights granted in this paragraph shall also be afforded the opportunity to displace other employees in accordance with this paragraph and the exercise of seniority hereunder.

(c) In the operation of (a) and (b) above, a senior employee has the prerogative of accepting layoff instead of displacing a junior employee, if he or she so desires.

(d) The Company will post a notice of layoff expected to last more than four (4) days at least ten (10) days in advance of such layoff, unless the conditions leading to such layoff resulted from an Act of God, labor dispute, or other condition beyond the control of the Company.

Section 2. (a) Employees affected by a reduction of forces shall be recalled to their regular job classification and department in the inverse order of the force reduction. If the employee refuses such recall, he will be terminated as a voluntary quit. Employees recalled to their regular job classification and department, but not to their regular shift, shall be returned to their regular shift in order of seniority as openings occur.

(b) When a vacancy exists after exhausting paragraph (a), the job will be posted for bid according to the bidding procedure. If no employee is awarded such job vacancy, the most senior employee on layoff shall be afforded the vacancy providing he or she has the skill and ability to perform the work.

Section 3. Nothing in this Agreement shall prohibit the Company's laying off the employees for the purpose of taking inventory and offering the work available during such period to the senior qualified employees in the department.

XII. EMPLOYEE SAFETY

Section 1. The Company agrees to provide a place of employment which shall be safe for the employees therein, shall furnish and use safety devices and safeguards, and shall adopt and use methods and processes adequate to render such places of employment safe. The term "safe" or "safety" as applied to employment or place of employment shall include conditions and methods of sanitation and hygiene necessary for the protection of life, health and safety of the employees.

Section 2. The Company agrees that all machinery, equipment and facilities the Company furnishes shall meet with all required legal standards of safety and sanitation. Accident records shall be kept and maintained by the Company and shall be made available on request to the Safety Committee.

Section 3. The Company agrees to maintain a Joint Labor-Management Safety Committee. The Safety Committee shall be composed of at least two (2) representatives of Management and at least two (2) representatives of the Union. The Union representatives shall be selected by the local Union. The Safety Committee shall be able to sit in on any safety investigation when any employee is questioned and shall:

Meet at least once every month on definitely established dates;

Make inspections of the plant at least once every month;

Make recommendations for the correction of unsafe or harmful work practices;

Review and analyze all reports of industrial injury and illness, investigate causes of same and recommend rules and procedures for the prevention of accidents and disease and for the promotion of health and safety of employees;

Promote health and safety education.

Section 4. All disputes and disagreements brought to the attention of the Safety Committee, arising under the Safety clause of this contract, if not disposed of by the Safety Committee, shall be subject to the Grievance Procedure.

Section 5. In the event of special circumstances, the Safety Committee may seek advice, opinion and suggestions of experts and authorities on safety matters. Such experts shall have access to the plant for the purpose of applying this article at any time upon providing reasonable notice. The Personnel Manager or his/her designee and a Union designee shall accompany the Safety representative.

Section 6. Employees injured in the plant shall be furnished medical aid or treatment on Company time, and shall receive full pay for the shift on which they were working when injured.

Section 7. The Union agrees to participate on the Safety Committee and will endeavor to have its members observe all safety rules and use all equipment and safeguards provided. The Union representative on the Safety Committee, upon request, shall be allowed to leave his or her work during working hours for the purpose of performing his or duties as outlined in this Article without loss of time or pay.

XIII. DISCIPLINE

Section 1. The Employer may not discipline or discharge except for just cause and only after due regard for principles of progressive discipline, except as specified otherwise herein.

Section 2. The following shall be causes for immediate discharge:

(a) Bringing intoxicants, narcotics or other dangerous drugs into or consuming intoxicants or such narcotics or drugs in the plant or on the plant premises.

(b) Reporting for duty under the influence of liquor, narcotics or drugs.

(c) Smoking while on duty or in prohibited areas.

(d) Deliberate destruction or removal of Company's or another employee's property.

(e) Refusal to comply with Company rules, provided that such rules shall be posted in a conspicuous place where they may be read by all employees; and further provided that no changes in present rules or no additional rules shall be made that are inconsistent with this Agreement.

(f) Disorderly conduct.

(g) Sleeping on duty.

(h) Giving or taking a bribe of any nature, as an inducement to obtaining work or retaining a position.

(i) Failure to report for duty without bona fide reasons.

(j) Reading of books, magazines or newspapers while on duty except where required in line of duty.

(k) Unsanitary practice endangering the health of others.

(*l*) Gambling during working hours.

Section 3. Except for the infractions noted in Section 2, above, the Employer shall not discharge or suspend an employee without first having discussed such action with the employee and Shop Steward or, in absence of both, having given notice to the Union. Such notice may be by telephone, telegram, or letter, and such notice must include the reason or reasons for an employee's discharge or suspension.

Section 4. No employee in the bargaining unit shall be required to take any polygraph test, but an employee may, of his own volition, take such a test.

XIV. GRIEVANCE PROCEDURE

Section 1. Should grievances arise, a diligent effort shall be made to settle all grievances as soon as possible after they have been presented either by the Union or an employee.

Any employee having a grievance shall submit same in writing as promptly as possible after its occurrence but no grievance shall be valid if not presented within fifteen (15) days from the time the cause for complaint became known to the employee.

If at any time a grievance remains at any step below Step 4 for more than seven (7) working days, the Local Union may, by written notice to local management, request that such grievance be heard at the next step.

Section 2. When grievances arise, the following steps shall be followed, each to be exhausted before resorting to the next:

Step 1. Between the immediate supervisor and the aggrieved employee; the appropriate Union representative shall be given an opportunity to be present.

Step 2. Between the Production Superintendent and the Union Committee.

Step 3. Between the Operations Manager and the Union Committee.

Step 4. Between the Divisional Vice President of the Company, or his representative, and the President of the International Union, or his representative.

XV. ARBITRATION

Section 1. In the event that a grievance based upon the interpretation, application or compliance with the terms of this Agreement shall not have been satisfactorily settled, the Union within thirty (30) days after the Company's answer to the last step in the grievance procedure may submit the matter to the American Arbitration Association under their rules then in effect. Expenses of the arbitrator shall be shared equally by the Company and the Union. The decision of the arbitrator shall be binding upon both parties to this Agreement. Such decision shall be within the scope and terms of this Agreement, but shall not change any of its terms or conditions.

XVI. STRIKES AND LOCKOUTS

Section 1. The Union and the Company agree that there shall be no strikes, sympathy strikes, boycotts, lockouts or general slowing down of production by employees, during the life of this Agreement, and that in the event differences should arise between the Company and the Union or its members employed by the Company, as to the meaning and application of this Agreement, or should any local trouble of any kind arise in the plant, there shall be no suspension of work by the employees on account of such differences.

XVII. EMPLOYEE BENEFITS

The benefits as shown in this section shall continue in effect during the life of this Agreement.

Medical Insurance: Blue Cross Preferred Comprehensive; Blue Shield, 100; and Major Medical Insurance shall continue to be provided at Company expense for employees until age 70. The Major Medical Insurance referred to herein shall be provided on the basis of $10,000 maximum; $100 deductible per person, and 80/20 participation.

A Blue Shield Eye Examination and Refraction Program shall be provided for employees and certain of their dependents at Company expense as promptly as arrangements can be made.

Dental Insurance: A dental insurance plan to be agreed upon by the parties shall be effective April 1, 2017. This plan shall provide dental benefits for employees and their covered dependents. Company shall contribute $20.00 per month per covered employee toward the cost of this coverage and any excess cost shall be made up by employee contributions.

Death in Family: Should death occur to the Mother, Father, Stepmother, Stepfather, Wife, Children, Stepchildren, Sister or Brother of any employee, he or she shall be entitled to a three-day leave of absence and should death occur to the Grandparent of any employee he or she shall be entitled to a one-day leave of absence. For all such leaves of absence the employee will be paid at his or her straight-time rate provided the leave is taken during the normal week, i.e., Monday through Friday.

Jury Duty: The Company agrees to pay to any employee who shall serve on a bona fide jury panel an amount equal to the difference between the employee's earnings from such service and his or her regular eight (8) hours straight time pay for the days, not in excess of fifteen days for any single period of jury service, during which the employee shall be absent and on jury service.

Sick Benefits: Provision is made for the payment of Sick Benefits to hourly paid employees who have been on the payroll for not less than one year immediately prior to the event of sickness.

On presentation of a licensed physician's, dentist's, chiropodist's, or chiropractor's certificate, an employee who has been ill seven (7) or more consecutive days is entitled to an amount equal to fifty (50) percent of his or her forty-hour weekly wages or the amount to which the employee would be entitled under the State Temporary Disability Law, whichever is greater, from the day he became ill, for a period not in excess of twenty-six weeks in any twelve-month period.

Sick benefits have no connection with illness due to injury in the plant. Disabilities due to injuries in the plant are compensated for under Employers' Liability Insurance in accordance with State regulations.

Retirement: All employees covered by this Agreement are also covered by the Pension Plan which went into operation July 1, 1990, as amended: This is a funded pension plan.

A copy of the Summary Plan Description will be regularly furnished to each new employee. Additional copies may be obtained upon request at the Personnel Office.

Life Insurance: A group life insurance policy will be purchased by the Company so that each employee with one or more years of continuous service with the Company shall have life insurance protection in the amount of $10,000 in the event such employee shall die while employed by the Company and before such employee's retirement. Beneficiary designations shall be made by each such employee in accordance with the provisions of such group policy.

XVIII. NEW EMPLOYEES

Section 1. New employees shall be considered probationary employees and shall not rank for seniority until they shall have been in the employ of the Company for sixty (60) calendar days, unless otherwise extended by mutual agreement. After the expiration of the sixty (60) day period, they shall cease to be probationary employees and rates of pay and all other provisions of this Agreement shall be applicable to them. They shall then rank for seniority from the date of original hiring in the plant. During the probationary period the Company may pay the employee the regular job wage rate.

XIX. SCOPE OF WORK; NEW TECHNOLOGIES

Section 1. It is the intent of the parties to permit the Company to remain technologically competitive and to meet its customer's needs so long as work opportunities now and in the future are preserved for the employees within the bargaining unit identified in Article II. As new technologies develop, the parties pledge their best efforts to fully train and include bargaining unit employees in the implementation of such technologies.

Section 2. In furtherance of the parties' intent, a technology committee consisting of two (2) Union and two (2) Company representatives shall be established and shall meet at the request of either the Union or the Company. The committee shall be empowered to investigate and discuss all issues involving the impact of new technology on bargaining unit work. The committee shall reach agreement on issues investigated and discussed.

Section 3. The Company shall provide training, if required, on any new technology used to perform bargaining unit work. The Company will not permit its proprietary or licensed software, data, hardware, equipment or facilities to be used by others to perform work or functions that replace work or functions being performed by bargaining unit employees.

XX. COMPLETE AGREEMENT

Section 1. The parties hereto acknowledge that, during the negotiations which resulted in this Agreement, each had the unlimited right and opportunity to make demands and proposals with respect to any subject or matter not removed by law from the area of collective bargaining, and that the understandings and Agreements arrived at by the parties after the exercise of the right and opportunity are set forth in this Agreement. Therefore, the parties hereto, for the life of this Agreement, each voluntarily and unqualifiedly waives the right, and each expressly agrees that the other shall not be obligated, to bargain collectively with respect to any subject or matter referred to, or covered or not specifically referred to or covered in the Agreement, even though such subject or matter may not have been within the knowledge or contemplation of either or both of the parties at the time that they negotiated or signed this Agreement.

Section 2. The parties hereto expressly agree that this contract is the sole and complete Agreement between them and that any other previous understandings or Agreements, oral or written (inconsistent with the provisions of this Agreement), are superseded and are of no effect during the term of this Agreement (except as elsewhere provided in the Agreement).

XXI. TERM OF AGREEMENT

Section 1. This Agreement shall be effective April 1, 2020, and shall continue in full force and effect to and including March 31, 2023, and from year to year after the latter date, unless and until either of the parties hereto shall give to the other three (3) months' written notice prior to the end of the original term, or three (3) months' written notice prior to the end of any subsequent year, of an intention to modify or terminate at the end of the original term or of the then current year.

XXII. SUCCESSORS AND ASSIGNS

Section 1. This Agreement shall be binding upon the successors, purchasers, transferees and assignees of the Company.

Section 2. The Company shall give notice of the existence of this Agreement to any successor, purchaser, transferee or assignee. Such notice shall be in writing, with a copy to the Union, at least sixty (60) days in advance of the effective date of transfer. After such notice is given, upon the request of either party, the parties shall bargain in good faith about any matter not covered by this Agreement.

Exhibit A

All incumbent employees shall receive the following wages:

Effective June 1, 2020

Work Level A	Start	$12.71	–$16.06
Work Level B	Start	$13.64	–$17.02
Work Level C	Start	$14.53	–$18.48
Work Level D	Start	$15.01	–$18.96
Work Level E	Start	$17.15	–$21.10

Effective June 1, 2021

Work Level A	Start	$12.88	–$16.34
Work Level B	Start	$13.83	–$17.32
Work Level C	Start	$14.74	–$18.81
Work Level D	Start	$15.23	–$19.30
Work Level E	Start	$17.41	–$21.48

Effective June 1, 2022

Work Level A	Start	$13.20	–$16.84
Work Level B	Start	$14.18	–$17.86
Work Level C	Start	$15.12	–$19.40
Work Level D	Start	$15.62	–$19.91
Work Level E	Start	$17.88	–$22.16

MEMORANDUM OF UNDERSTANDING #1
ABSENTEE CONTROL PROGRAM

Executed by Company and Union on June 1, 2007

The Company shall have the sole option of placing an employee on the absentee watch list by issuing a written notice to the employee, with a copy to the Union. The Company's decision to place an employee on the absentee watch list shall not be subject to the grievance or arbitration provisions of the contract.

Once an employee is placed on the absentee watch list, termination will take place in the event there are two (2) unexcused absences or four (4) tardinesses, or any combination thereof in any rolling 90-calendar day period. An unexcused absence is defined as *any* absence that is not approved by the Company in writing and signed by the Company President or a designee. In the event a termination based upon absenteeism or tardiness is processed to arbitration, the arbitrator shall be limited to determining whether or not an individual had two (2) or more unexcused absences or four (4) or more tardinesses, or any combination thereof, in the rolling 90-day period. It is further understood that an individual placed on the absentee watch list shall remain on that list for 300 calendar days provided there is no intervening unexcused absence or tardiness and otherwise for 365 calendar days from the date of written notice provided for above.

MEMORANDUM OF UNDERSTANDING #2
CHEMICAL SUBSTANCE ABUSE POLICY

Executed by Company and Union on October 15, 2019

1. An employee who is found or reasonable believed to be under the influence of alcohol, drugs or an intoxicant in the employee's system during the course of business on Company premises or when conducting Company business *at any time* will be subject to discipline including discharge, or may be referred to the Employee Assistance Program. Being "under the influence" of alcohol is defined as a blood alcohol content of .04 or higher; and being "under the influence" of an unauthorized controlled substance, illegal drug, prescription, or non-prescription drug is defined as testing positive at specified ng/ml levels.

2. It is the responsibility of each employee to report promptly to the Medical Department the use or possession of any prescribed medication which may affect judgment, performance, or behavior. No prescription drug will be brought on the Company premises or business in any manner, combination, or quantity other than that prescribed by a licensed physician. Failure to comply may result in discipline, including discharge, or the employee may be referred to the Employee Assistance Program.

3. All new hires will be tested for the use of drugs, alcohol, and intoxicating substances. Refusal to submit to testing, or testing positive, will result in rejection of employment by the Company. Applicants who

are denied employment because of a positive test result may reapply for employment and be re-tested after one year from the time of initial rejection.

4. If Management has reasonable suspicion (as herein defined) that an employee is under the influence or, impaired by, or unfit for work due to a chemical substance, including but not limited to a drug, alcohol, or intoxicating substance, or in the event of an accident when the cause may be human error, the subject employee shall be required to submit to medical chemical screening, which may include breath, saliva, urine, and/or blood specimen testing. Positive test results may result in the employee being disciplined, up to and including discharge, or the employee may be referred to the Employee Assistance Program.

5. "Reasonable suspicion" means objective belief based upon reasonable, individualized suspicion that can be described with particularity that a specific employee may be under the influence of alcohol, drugs, or other intoxicating substances based on direct observation by a supervisor or management representative.

are denied employment because of a positive test result may reapply for employment and be re-tested after one year from the date of initial rejection.

11. If Management has reasonable suspicion (as herein defined) that an employee is under the influence of, impaired by, or unfit for work due to a chemical substance including but not limited to a drug, alcohol, or intoxicating substance, or in the event of an accident which the cause may be human error, the subject employee shall be required to submit to medical evaluation screening, which may include breath, urine, and/or [illegible] testing. Positive test results may result in the [illegible] of the [illegible]

[illegible]

reasonable, individualized suspicion that can be described with particularity that a specific employee may be under the influence of alcohol, drugs, or other intoxicating substances based on direct observation by a supervisor or management representative.

National Labor Relations Board Forms

(1) Petition for Election.

(2) Stipulated Election Agreement, and

(3) Unfair Labor Practice Charge Against Employer.

(4) Unfair Labor Practice Charge Against Union.

(5) Remedial Notice.

FORM EXEMPT UNDER 44 U.S.C

INTERNET
FORM NLRB-502
(2-08)

UNITED STATES GOVERNMENT
NATIONAL LABOR RELATIONS BOARD
PETITION

DO NOT WRITE IN THIS SPACE	
Case No.	Date Filed

INSTRUCTIONS: Submit an original of this Petition to the NLRB Regional Office in the Region in which the employer concerned is located.

The Petitioner alleges that the following circumstances exist and requests that the NLRB proceed under its proper authority pursuant to Section 9 of the NLRA.

1. PURPOSE OF THIS PETITION (If box RC, RM, or RD is checked and a charge under Section 8(b)(7) of the Act has been filed involving the Employer named herein, the statement following the description of the type of petition shall not be deemed made.) (Check One)

☐ **RC-CERTIFICATION OF REPRESENTATIVE** - A substantial number of employees wish to be represented for purposes of collective bargaining by Petitioner and Petitioner desires to be certified as representative of the employees.

☐ **RM-REPRESENTATION (EMPLOYER PETITION)** - One or more individuals or labor organizations have presented a claim to Petitioner to be recognized as the representative of employees of Petitioner.

☐ **RD-DECERTIFICATION (REMOVAL OF REPRESENTATIVE) - A substantial number of employees assert that the certified or currently recognized bargaining representative is no longer their representative.**

☐ **UD-WITHDRAWAL OF UNION SHOP AUTHORITY (REMOVAL OF OBLIGATION TO PAY DUES)** - Thirty percent (30%) or more of employees in a bargaining unit covered by an agreement between their employer and a labor organization desire that such authority be rescinded.

☐ **UC-UNIT CLARIFICATION**- A labor organization is currently recognized by Employer, but Petitioner seeks clarification of placement of certain employees: (Check one) ☐ In unit not previously certified. ☐ In unit previously certified in Case No. ____________

☐ **AC-AMENDMENT OF CERTIFICATION**- Petitioner seeks amendment of certification issued in Case No. ____________
Attach statement describing the specific amendment sought.

2. Name of Employer	Employer Representative to contact	Tel. No.
3. Address(es) of Establishment(s) involved *(Street and number, city, State, ZIP code)*		Fax No.
4a. Type of Establishment (Factory, mine, wholesaler, etc.)	4b. Identify principal product or service	Cell No.
		e-Mail
5. Unit Involved *(In UC petition, describe present bargaining unit and attach description of proposed clarification.)*		6a. Number of Employees in Unit:
Included		Present
Excluded		Proposed *(By UC/AC)*
		6b. Is this petition supported by 30% or more of the employees in the unit?* ☐ Yes ☐ No *Not applicable in RM, UC, and AC

(If you have checked box RC in 1 above, check and complete EITHER item 7a or 7b, whichever is applicable)

7a. ☐ Request for recognition as Bargaining Representative was made on (Date) ____________ and Employer declined recognition on or about (Date) ____________ (If no reply received, so state).

7b. ☐ Petitioner is currently recognized as Bargaining Representative and desires certification under the Act.

8. Name of Recognized or Certified Bargaining Agent *(If none, so state.)*		Affiliation	
Address	Tel. No.	Date of Recognition or Certification	
	Cell No.	Fax No.	e-Mail

9. Expiration Date of Current Contract. If any *(Month, Day, Year)*	10. If you have checked box UD in 1 above, show here the date of execution of agreement granting union shop *(Month, Day and Year)*
11a. Is there now a strike or picketing at the Employer's establishment(s) involved? Yes ☐ No ☐	11b. If so, approximately how many employees are participating?

11c. The Employer has been picketed by or on behalf of *(Insert Name)* ____________, a labor organization, of *(Insert Address)* ____________ Since *(Month, Day, Year)* ____________

12. Organizations or individuals other than Petitioner (and other than those named in items 8 and 11c), which have claimed recognition as representatives and other organizations and individuals known to have a representative interest in any employees in unit described in item 5 above. (If none, so state)

Name	Address	Tel. No.	Fax No.
		Cell No.	e-Mail

13. Full name of party filing petition (If labor organization, give full name, including local name and number)

14a. Address *(street and number, city, state, and ZIP code)*	14b. Tel. No. EXT	14c. Fax No.
	14d. Cell No.	14e. e-Mail

15. Full name of national or international labor organization of which Petitioner is an affiliate or constituent *(to be filled in when petition is filed by a labor organization)*

I declare that I have read the above petition and that the statements are true to the best of my knowledge and belief.

Name *(Print)*	Signature	Title *(if any)*
Address *(street and number, city, state, and ZIP code)*	Tel. No.	Fax No.
	Cell No.	eMail

WILLFUL FALSE STATEMENTS ON THIS PETITION CAN BE PUNISHED BY FINE AND IMPRISONMENT (U.S. CODE, TITLE 18, SECTION 1001)

PRIVACY ACT STATEMENT

Solicitation of the information on this form is authorized by the National Labor Relations Act (NLRA), 29 U.S.C. § 151 *et seq.* The principal use of the information is to assist the National Labor Relations Board (NLRB) in processing unfair labor practice and related proceedings or litigation. The routine uses for the information are fully set forth in the Federal Register, 71 Fed. Reg. 74942-43 (Dec. 13, 2006). The NLRB will further explain these uses upon request. Disclosure of this information to the NLRB is voluntary; however, failure to supply the information will cause the NLRB to decline to invoke its processes.

FORM NLRB-652
(4-95)

UNITED STATES OF AMERICA
NATIONAL LABOR RELATIONS BOARD
STIPULATED ELECTION AGREEMENT

The parties agree that a hearing is waived, that approval of this Agreement constitutes withdrawal of any notice of hearing previously issued in this matter, that the petition is amended to conform to this Agreement, and further **AGREE AS FOLLOWS:**

1. **SECRET BALLOT.** A secret-ballot election shall be held under the supervision of the Regional Director in the unit defined below at the agreed time and place, under the Board's Rules and Regulations.

2. **ELIGIBLE VOTERS.** The eligible voters shall be unit employees employed during the payroll period for eligibility, including employees who did not work during that period because they were ill, on vacation, or temporarily laid off, employees engaged in an economic strike which commenced less than 12 months before the election date and who retained their status as such during the eligibility period and their replacements, and employees in the military services of the United States who appear in person at the polls. Ineligible to vote are employees who have quit or been discharged for cause since the payroll period for eligibility, employees engaged in a strike who have been discharged for cause since the commencement thereof and who have not been rehired or reinstated before the election date, and employees engaged in an economic strike which commenced more than 12 months before the election date and who have been permanently replaced. The Employer shall provide to the Regional Director, within 7 days after the Regional Director has approved this Agreement, an election eligibility list containing the full names and addresses of all eligible voters. *Excelsior Underwear, Inc.*, 156 NLRB 1236 (1966). *North Macon Health Care Facility*, 315 NLRB 359 (1994).

3. **NOTICE OF ELECTION.** Copies of the Notice of Election shall be posted by the Employer in conspicuous places and usual posting places easily accessible to the voters at least three (3) full working days prior to 12:01 a.m. of the day of the election. As soon as the election arrangements are finalized, the Employer will be informed when the Notices must be posted in order to comply with the posting requirement. Failure to post the Election Notices as required shall be grounds for setting aside the election whenever proper and timely objections are filed.

4. **ACCOMMODATIONS REQUIRED.** All parties should notify the Regional Director as soon as possible of any voters, potential voters, or other participants in this election who have handicaps falling within the provisions of Section 504 of the Rehabilitation Act of 1973, as amended, and 29 C.F.R. 100.603, and who in order to participate in this election need appropriate auxiliary aids, as defined in 29 C.F.R. 100.603, and request the necessary assistance.

5. **OBSERVERS.** Each party may station an equal number of authorized, nonsupervisory-employee observers at the polling places to assist in the election, to challenge the eligibility of voters, and to verify the tally.

6. **TALLY OF BALLOTS.** Upon conclusion of the election, the ballots will be counted and a tally of ballots prepared and immediately made available to the parties.

7. **POSTELECTION AND RUNOFF PROCEDURES.** All procedures after the ballots are counted shall conform with the Board's Rules and Regulations.

8. **RECORD.** The record in this case shall include this Agreement and be governed by the Board's Rules and Regulations.

(Over)

9. **COMMERCE.** The Employer is engaged in commerce within the meaning of Section 2(6) and (7) of the National Labor Relations Act and a question affecting commerce has arisen concerning the representation of employees within the meaning of Section 9(c). (Insert commerce facts.)

10. **WORDING ON THE BALLOT.** When only one labor organization is on the ballot, the choice shall be "Yes" or "No." If more than one labor organization is on the ballot, the choices shall appear as follows, reading left to right or top to bottom. (*If more than one labor organization is on the ballot, any labor organization may have its name removed by the approval of the Regional Director of a timely written request.*)

First.

Second.

Third.

11. PAYROLL PERIOD FOR ELIGIBILITY - THE PERIOD ENDING ______________________

12. DATE, HOURS, AND PLACE OF ELECTION.

13. THE APPROPRIATE COLLECTIVE-BARGAINING UNIT.

______________________ *(Employer)*	______________________ *(Labor Organization)*
By ______________________ *(Name)* *(Date)*	By ______________________ *(Name)* *(Date)*
______________________ *(Title)*	______________________ *(Title)*
Recommended:	
______________________ *(Board Agent)* *(Date)*	
Date approved ______________________	______________________ *(Labor Organization)*
______________________ Regional Director National Labor Relations Board	By ______________________ *(Name)* *(Date)*
Case ______________________	______________________ *(Title)*

INTERNET
FORM NLRB-501
(2-08)

UNITED STATES OF AMERICA
NATIONAL LABOR RELATIONS BOARD
CHARGE AGAINST EMPLOYER

FORM EXEMPT UNDER 44 U.S.C 3512

DO NOT WRITE IN THIS SPACE	
Case	Date Filed

INSTRUCTIONS:
File an original with NLRB Regional Director for the region in which the alleged unfair labor practice occurred or is occurring.

1. EMPLOYER AGAINST WHOM CHARGE IS BROUGHT

a. Name of Employer		b. Tel. No.
		c. Cell No.
d. Address *(Street, city, state, and ZIP code)*	e. Employer Representative	f. Fax No.
		g. e-Mail
		h. Number of workers employed
i. Type of Establishment *(factory, mine, wholesaler, etc.)*	j. Identify principal product or service	

k. The above-named employer has engaged in and is engaging in unfair labor practices within the meaning of section 8(a), subsections (1) and *(list subsections)* of the National Labor Relations Act, and these unfair labor practices are practices affecting commerce within the meaning of the Act, or these unfair labor practices are unfair practices affecting commerce within the meaning of the Act and the Postal Reorganization Act.

2. Basis of the Charge *(set forth a clear and concise statement of the facts constituting the alleged unfair labor practices)*

3. Full name of party filing charge *(if labor organization, give full name, including local name and number)*

4a. Address *(Street and number, city, state, and ZIP code)*	4b. Tel. No.
	4c. Cell No.
	4d. Fax No.
	4e. e-Mail

5. Full name of national or international labor organization of which it is an affiliate or constituent unit *(to be filled in when charge is filed by a labor organization)*

6. DECLARATION
I declare that I have read the above charge and that the statements are true to the best of my knowledge and belief.

By ______________________ ______________________
(signature of representative or person making charge) *(Print/type name and title or office, if any)*

Address ______________________ ______________ *(date)*

Tel. No.
Office, if any, Cell No.
Fax No.
e-Mail

WILLFUL FALSE STATEMENTS ON THIS CHARGE CAN BE PUNISHED BY FINE AND IMPRISONMENT (U.S. CODE, TITLE 18, SECTION 1001)

PRIVACY ACT STATEMENT

Solicitation of the information on this form is authorized by the National Labor Relations Act (NLRA), 29 U.S.C. § 151 *et seq.* The principal use of the information is to assist the National Labor Relations Board (NLRB) in processing unfair labor practice and related proceedings or litigation. The routine uses for the information are fully set forth in the Federal Register, 71 Fed. Reg. 74942-43 (Dec. 13, 2006). The NLRB will further explain these uses upon request. Disclosure of this information to the NLRB is voluntary; however, failure to supply the information will cause the NLRB to decline to invoke its processes.

FORM EXEMPT UNDER 44 U.S.C 3512

INTERNET
FORM NLRB-508
(2-08)

UNITED STATES OF AMERICA
NATIONAL LABOR RELATIONS BOARD
CHARGE AGAINST LABOR ORGANIZATION OR ITS AGENTS

DO NOT WRITE IN THIS SPACE	
Case	Date Filed

INSTRUCTIONS. File an original with NLRB Regional Director for the region in which the alleged unfair labor practice occurred or is occurring.

1. LABOR ORGANIZATION OR ITS AGENTS AGAINST WHICH CHARGE IS BROUGHT

a. Name	b. Union Representative to contact	
c. Address *(Street, city, state, and ZIP code)*	d. Tel. No.	e. Cell No.
	f. Fax No.	g. e-Mail

h. The above-named organization(s) or its agents has *(have)* engaged in and is *(are)* engaging in unfair labor practices within the meaning of section 8(b), subsection(s) *(list subsections)* of the National Labor Relations Act, and these unfair labor practices are unfair practices affecting commerce within the meaning of the Act, or these unfair labor practices are unfair practices affecting commerce within the meaning of the Act and the Postal Reorganization Act.

2. Basis of the Charge *(set forth a clear and concise statement of the facts constituting the alleged unfair labor practices)*

3. Name of Employer	4a. Tel. No.	b. Cell No.
	c. Fax No.	d. e-Mail
5. Location of plant involved *(street, city, state and ZIP code)*	6. Employer representative to contact	
7. Type of establishment *(factory, mine, wholesaler, etc.)*	8. Identify principal product or service	9. Number of workers employed
10. Full name of party filing charge	11a. Tel. No.	b. Cell No.
	c. Fax No.	d. e-Mail
11. Address of party filing charge *(street, city, state and ZIP code.)*		

12. DECLARATION

I declare that I have read the above charge and that the statements therein are true to the best of my knowledge and belief.

By ______________________________ ______________________________
(signature of representative or person making charge) *(Print/type name and title or office, if any)*

Address ______________________________ *(date)*__________

Tel. No.
Cell No.
Fax No.
e-Mail

WILLFUL FALSE STATEMENTS ON THIS CHARGE CAN BE PUNISHED BY FINE AND IMPRISONMENT (U.S. CODE, TITLE 18, SECTION 1001)

PRIVACY ACT STATEMENT

Solicitation of the information on this form is authorized by the National Labor Relations Act (NLRA), 29 U.S.C. § 151 et seq. The principal use of the information is to assist the National Labor Relations Board (NLRB) in processing unfair labor practice and related proceedings or litigation. The routine uses for the information are fully set forth in the Federal Register, 71 Fed. Reg. 74942-43 (Dec. 13, 2006). The NLRB will further explain these uses upon request. Disclosure of this information to the NLRB is voluntary; however, failure to supply the information will cause the NLRB to decline to invoke its processes.

NATIONAL LABOR RELATIONS BOARD

AN AGENCY OF THE UNITED STATES GOVERNMENT

The National Labor Relations Act gives employees these rights:

To engage in self-organization;
To form, join, or help unions;
To bargain collectively through a representative of their own choosing
To act together for collective bargaining or other mutual aid or protection;
To refrain from all of these things.

WE WILL NOT promulgate, maintain or enforce a rule which prohibits employees from posting pro-Union literature on Company bulletin boards without permission.

WE WILL NOT threaten employees with discipline for violating such a rule.

WE WILL NOT promulgate, maintain or enforce a rule which prohibits the distribution of materials related to union or other activity by Section 7 of the National Labor Relations Act in nonwork areas without prior approval

WE WILL NOT interrogate job applicants about their union affiliation, their feelings about working for a non-union employer or whether their past employers were unionized.

WE WILL NOT request employees to report to management if they are harassed by employees who support [Union], or any other labor organization.

WE WILL NOT refer to employees interested in or engaged in union activity as "trouble" and **WE WILL NOT** threaten to discharge such employees because of their union activities.

WE WILL NOT in any other manner interfere with, restrain or coerce employees in the exercise of the rights guaranteed by Section 7 of the Act.

WE WILL notify our employees, in writing, by memorandum or letter separate from this document, that the rules referred to above are no longer in effect.

WE WILL allow our employees to wear union and/or other buttons, insignia, stickers, writings or other markings on their clothing. We will not allow our employees to put union or other buttons, insignia, stickers, writings or other markings on their hard hats, except for safety and security items specifically required by the Company.

WE WILL amend our rule with respect to hard hats to specify that the only items permitted to be put on the hard hats are safety and security items specifically required by the Company. **WE WILL NOT** promulgate, maintain or enforce a rule which allows any other items.

XYZ COMPANY, INC.
(Employer)

Dated: ____________________ By ______________________________
(Representative) (Title)

THIS IS AN OFFICIAL NOTICE AND MUST NOT BE DEFACED BY ANYONE

This notice must remain posted for 60 consecutive days from the date of posting and must not be altered, defaced, or covered by any other material. Any questions concerning this notice or compliance with its provisions may be directed to the Board's Office,

615 Chestnut Street, One Independence Mall, 7th Floor,
Philadelphia, Pennsylvania 19106 (215) 597-7601

Notice may be posted in a language other than English when commonly spoken by the workforce. In Durham School Services, 360 N.L.R.B. No. 85 (2014), a unanimous five-member Board ordered that in all future cases the notice will include a hyperlink to a copy of the decision on the Board's website. Even if employees cannot use the hyperlink, it will give them an electronic address where they can obtain a copy of the decision for those employees who do not have access to or do not wish to use a computer to obtain an electronic copy of the decision, the notice also will provide an address to which they may write, and a telephone number which they may call, to obtain a printed copy of the decision from the Board's Executive Secretary.

will provide an address to which they may write, and a telephone number which they may call, to obtain a printed copy of the decision from the Board's Executive Secretary.

PART ONE

THE EVOLUTION OF LABOR RELATIONS LAWS

II. JURISDICTION, ORGANIZATION AND PROCEDURE OF THE NLRB

A. NLRB JURISDICTION

3. EXCLUDED EMPLOYEES

Page 68. Add before Questions for Discussion:

In a notice issued on December 27, 2021 in *The Atlanta Opera, Inc.*, 371 NLRB No. 45 (2021), the Board invited parties and amici to submit briefs addressing whether the Board should reconsider its standard for determining the independent contractor status of workers articulated in *SuperShuttle.* On June 13, 2023, the Board issued its opinion in the case, indeed overruling *SuperShuttle* and returning to the standard set for in its 2014 *FedEx Home Delivery* decision. The Atlanta Opera, Inc., 372 NLRB No. 95. In applying the *FedEx II* standard, the Board found that the makeup artists, wig artists, and hairstylists who work at the Atlanta Opera are covered employees, not independent contractors excluded from the Act. Member Kaplan dissented from the portion of the decision that overruled *SuperShuttle*, but concurred with the three in the majority that the workers were employees of Atlantic Opera.

Thus, the Board rejected the core holding in *SuperShuttle* that entrepreneurial opportunity for gain or loss should be the "animating principle" of the independent-contractor test. In returning to the *FedEx II* standard, it emphasized entrepreneurial opportunity would be taken into account, along with the traditional common-law factors. In the majority's view, the common-law approach, which arguably is broader, will better ensure that workers are not improperly excluded from the Act's protections.

Given that the pendulum has now swung back to the *FedEx II* approach, consider the following *Questions for Discussion* in light of this ongoing debate.

Page 70. Add at the end of Note 3:

Now that the Board has abandoned the focus on entrepreneurial opportunity and returned to the more holistic common law test, the basis for the former GC's opinion on rideshare drivers has dissipated (at least for the moment). This will raise anew questions as to whether these drivers are employees under the Act. Perhaps this is a good time to take a fresh look at the drivers' status. Considering all of the circumstances and indicia of firm control and driver independence, as well as background policy arguments, should such drivers be deemed employees under the Act? Why or why not?

Page 75. Add following *Pacific Lutheran*:

In *University of So. Cal. v. NLRB*, 918 F.3d 126 (D.C. Cir. 2019), the court rejected the Board's decision that contingent faculty were not managerial because the contingent faculty participating in policy committees did not constitute a majority on such bodies. It is enough, the court opined, that they are "structurally included."

Page 76. Add after *Students on Athletic Scholarships*:

On September 29, 2021, General Counsel Abruzzo issued Memorandum GC 21–08, reinstating GC 17–01 (Jan. 31, 2017), which had stated the scholarship football players of Northwestern University and those similarly situated are employees with Section 7 rights, that misclassifying them should be submitted to the GC for advice as part of its decision to reconsider *Velox Express, Inc.*, 368 NLRB No. 61 (2019) (in which the Board refused to find a violation based on the employer having misclassified drivers as independent contractors), and that these players have the right to engage in concerted activity for mutual aid or protection. GC 21–08 and other recent GC memoranda are available here: https://www.nlrb.gov/guidance/memos-research/general-counsel-memos.

B. NLRB ORGANIZATION AND PROCEDURE

Page 78. Add to the end of the first paragraph:

The Third Circuit affirmed the long-accepted reading that the person alleging an unfair labor practice need not be a person adversely affected by the alleged wrong, one judge dissenting. FDRLST Media, LLC v. NLRB, 35 F.4th 108 (3d Cir. 2022).

Page 91. Add at the end of Subsection B:

On January 17, 2023, the D.C. Circuit affirmed the District Court as to three of the five provisions. *See* AFL-CIO v. NLRB, 57 F.4th 1023 (D.C. Cir. 2023). The provisions of the 2019 Final Rule the court found to be improperly enacted without notice and comment are (1) allowing employers up to five business days to furnish the voter list following the direction of election; (2) precluding Regional Directors from issuing certifications following elections if a request for review is pending or during the time in which a request for review could be filed; and (3) limiting a party's selection of election observers to individuals who are current members of the voting unit whenever possible. The Court of Appeals also found that a fourth amendment imposing an automatic impoundment of ballots under certain circumstances when a petition for review was pending with the Board, was contrary to Section 3(b) of the Act. It therefore vacated that portion of the Final Rule as well.

In light of the D.C. Circuit's ruling, on March 9, 2023, the Board issued a final rule rescinding the above four provisions and reinstating the previous regulations. The new rule also stays the effective date of two other provisions that had been enjoined by the District Court and have never gone into effect. These provisions had (1) allowed parties to litigate disputes over unit scope and voter eligibility prior to the election and (2) instructed Regional Directors not to schedule elections before the twentieth business day after the date of the direction of election. The Court of Appeals found that the Board could lawfully issue these provisions without notice and comment, but remanded the case to the District Court so that it could consider other grounds on which the provisions had been challenged. The Board stated that it will continue to postpone implementation of these provisions as litigation remains pending. Member Kaplan dissented from the issuance of the new rule.

C. THE SITUATION OF THE NLRB GOING FORWARD

Page 95. Add after the second full paragraph:

In his second day in office, President Biden terminated the Board's General Counsel, and his next in command. Mr. Peter Ohr, the Board's Regional Director in Chicago, was made Acting General Counsel. President Biden then nominated Jennifer Abruzzo to be General Counsel. On July 21, the Senate confirmed her 51–50, with Vice President Harris casting the tie-breaking vote. The President's power to remove the General Counsel has been affirmed in *Exla Enterprise Solutions, Inc. v. NLRB*, 32 F.4th 436 (5th Cir. 2022) and *NLRB v. Aakash, Inc.*, 58 F.4th 1099 (9th Cir. 2023).

The President also nominated two candidates for Board membership: Gwynne Wilcox, to the existing vacancy; David Prouty to succeed a Republican incumbent whose term ends in August. The Senate confirmed both nominees on July 28 in relatively close votes (52–47 and 53–46 respectively). The new members are well-known attorneys on the union side.

In the interregnum, the Board had announced that two current proposals for legal change were placed on hold: to allow employers to restrict access of union organizers to employer property and to restrict union access to voter eligibility lists.

On August 12, 2021, General Counsel Abruzzo issued Memorandum GC 21–04, setting out a long list of cases and subject matter areas that would be subject to the Office's "initiative" for change.

In light of the D.C. Circuit's ruling, on March 6, 2023, the Board issued a final rule rescinding the above four provisions and reinstating the previous regulations. The new rule also stays the effective date of two other provisions that had been enjoined by the District Court and have never gone into effect. These provisions had (1) allowed parties to litigate eligibility issues and were eligible prior to the election and (2) instructed Regional Directors not to schedule elections before the twentieth business day after the date of the direction of election. The Court of Appeals held that the Board [illegible] notice and comment, but remanded [illegible] Board [illegible] could consider [illegible].

[illegible] THE SITUATION OF THE NLRB GOING FORWARD

Page 80. Add after the second full paragraph:

In his second day in office, President Biden terminated the Board's General Counsel, and his assistant general counsel. Mr. Peter Ohr, the Board's Regional Director in Chicago, was made Acting General Counsel. President Biden then nominated Jennifer Abruzzo to be General Counsel. On July 21, the Senate confirmed her 51–50, with Vice President Harris casting the tie-breaking vote. The President's power to remove the General Counsel has been affirmed in *Exela Enterprise Solutions, Inc. v. NLRB*, 32 F.4th 436 (5th Cir. 2022), and *NLRB v. Aakash, Inc.*, 58 F.4th 1099 (9th Cir. 2023).

The President also nominated two candidates for Board membership: Gwynne Wilcox, to the existing vacancy; David Prouty, to succeed a Republican incumbent whose term ends in August. The Senate confirmed both nominees on July 28 in relatively close votes (52–47 and 53–46 respectively). The new members are well-known attorneys on the union side.

[illegible] the Board had announced that two current proposals for rule change were placed on hold: to allow employees to restrict access of union organizers to employer property and to restrict union access to voter eligibility lists.

On August 12, 2021, General Counsel Abruzzo issued Memorandum GC 21-04 setting out a long list of cases and subject matter areas that would be subject to the Office's "mandatory" for change.

PART TWO

THE ESTABLISHMENT OF THE COLLECTIVE BARGAINING RELATIONSHIP

I. PROTECTION OF THE RIGHT OF SELF-ORGANIZATION

A. INTERFERENCE, RESTRAINT AND COERCION

1. RESTRICTIONS ON SOLICITATION AND DISTRIBUTION

Page 105. Add at the end of Note 2:

In *Stabilus, Inc.*, 355 NLRB 836 (2010), the Board reiterated its rule that an employer must show "special circumstances" to warrant its enforcement of a policy that forbids the wearing of union insignia on company-required uniforms. In *Tesla, Inc.*, 370 NLRB No. 88 (2021), the Board's two-member Republican majority requested *amicus* briefs on the correctness of that standard. On "special circumstances," see *Constellation Brands U.S. v. NLRB*, 992 F.3d 642 (7th Cir. 2021).

Page 105. Add to Second Paragraph in Problem 3:

In *Tesla, Inc.*, 371 NLRB No. 131 (2022), in a 3–2 decision, the Board overruled *Wal-Mart Stores, Inc.*, 368 NLRB No. 146 (2019). It held *Republic Aviation* continued to govern the display of union insignia: the employer must prove "special circumstances" for the imposition of any restriction.

Page 125. Add at the end of the last paragraph in the note on Post-*Boeing* Developments:

Baylor Med. Center was followed in *Nichelson Terminal*, 369 NLRB No. 147 (2020), and *Int'l Game Technology*, 370 NLRB No. 50 (2020) ("IGT"). On how *Boeing* applies to confidentiality and social media policies, see *Medic Ambulance Service, Inc.*, 370 NLRB No. 65 (2021).

On February 23, 2023, the Board handed down *McLaren Macomb*, 372 NLRB No. 58, reversing its decisions in *Baylor University Medical Center* and *IGT*. In a 3–1 decision, the Board stated that it was returning to prior precedent holding that employers may not offer employees severance agreements that require the employees to broadly waive their Section 7 rights. Member Kaplan dissented.

The dispute in *McLaren Macomb* involved severance agreements offered to furloughed employees that prohibited them from making statements that could disparage the employer and from disclosing the terms of the agreement itself. The Board stated that an employer's offering employees a severance agreement that requires them to broadly give up their rights under Section 7 violates Section 8(a)(1). The offer of such a severance agreement is itself an attempt to deter employees from exercising their statutory rights, at a time when employees may feel they must give up these rights to secure the benefits provided in the agreement. The Board also observed that the agreement provided for substantial monetary and injunctive sanctions against the employee in the event the nondisparagement and confidentiality proscriptions were breached.

One month later, GC Abruzzo issued a memo to all field offices with guidance in light of *McLaren Macomb*, including on the decision's scope and effect. *See* Memorandum GC 23-05 (2023). Among other things, the memo provides guidance on the kinds of severance agreement provisions that could violate the Act, including those offering or including confidentiality, non-disclosure, and non-disparagement provisions. The GC made clear that lawful severance agreements may continue to be offered, but such agreements cannot contain overly broad provisions that affect or waive Section 7 rights, including engaging in protected concerted activities and accessing the NLRB.

In a notice issued on January 6, 2022, in *Stericycle, Inc.,* 371 NLRB No. 48 (2021), the Board invited parties and amici to submit briefs addressing, among other things, whether the Board should 1) continue to adhere to the standard adopted in *Boeing Co.*; 2) modify existing law to better ensure that the Board interprets work rules in a way that accounts for the economic dependence of workers and the potential chilling effect of a work rule on Section 7 rights, properly allocates the burden of proof in cases challenging the maintenance of a work rule, and appropriately balances employees' rights and employers' legitimate business interests; and 3) continue to hold that certain categories of work rules are always lawful to maintain. The three Democratic Members of the Board joined in issuing the notice and invitation while the two Republican members dissented. The news release linking to the notice can be found here: https://www.nlrb.gov/news-outreach/news-story/nlrb-invites-briefs-regarding-work-rules-standard.

On May 30, 2023, under the standard she urged above in *Stericycle*, General Counsel Abruzzo sent Memorandum GC 23-08 to all Regional Directors, Officers-in-Charge, and Resident Officers, setting forth her view that, except in limited circumstances, the proffer, maintenance, and enforcement of noncompete provisions in employment contracts and severance agreements violate Section 7 because they chill employees from exercising their rights to take collective action to improve their working conditions. She argues that overbroad non-compete agreements interfere with employees' ability to 1) concertedly threaten to resign to secure better working conditions; 2) carry out concerted threats to resign or otherwise concertedly resign to secure improved working conditions; 3) concertedly seek or accept employment with a local competitor to obtain better working conditions; 4) solicit their co-workers to go work for a local competitor as part of a broader course of protected concerted activity; and 5) seek employment, at least in part, to specifically engage in protected activity, including union organizing, with other workers at an employer's workplace. This is because such provisions could reasonably be construed by employees to deny them the ability to quit or change jobs by cutting off their access to other employment. Among other things, workers know that they will have greater difficulty replacing their lost income if they are discharged for exercising their statutory rights to organize and act together to improve working conditions.

The memo acknowledges that noncompete agreements could be lawful if they restrict only individuals' managerial or ownership interests in a competing business, or true independent-contractor relationships. There also may be circumstances in which a narrowly tailored non-compete agreement's infringement on employee rights may be justified by special circumstances. The memo further notes that the GC is committed to an interagency approach to restrictions on the exercise of employee rights, including with the Federal Trade Commission and Department of Justice's Antitrust Division, both of which have acted to address the anticompetitive effects of non-compete agreements. The news release linking to the notice can be found here: https://www.nlrb.gov/news-outreach/news-story/nlrb-general-counsel-issues-memo-on-non-competes-violating-the-national.

Page 135. Add after *Lechmere*, above the Problems for Discussion:

On June 23, 2021, the Supreme Court handed down *Cedar Point Nursery v. Hassid*, 141 S. Ct. 2063 (2021). California's Agricultural Labor Relations Act of 1975 allows unions a right of access by two union organizers on the employer's premises, subject to crew size, for an hour before and after work and a one hour lunch break for a total of 30 days in a calendar year and subject to other restrictions. The Court held, 6 to 3, this access rule to be an unconstitutional "taking" of property without compensation. The majority distinguished *Babcock & Wilcox* as a "highly contingent access right" allowed in a case where "taking" was not argued. It also distinguished a "trespass" from a "taking": when the former is merely occasional it is not a "taking" and it distinguished cases concerning "longstanding background restrictions on property rights" and "traditional common law privilege to access private property." It opined that none of these categories apply to the vindication of the public policy affording workers a right to form, join, or assist a labor organization. Justices Breyer, Sotomayor, and Kagan dissented.

Page 136. Add at end of Problem 5:

The *Tobin Center* decision was denied enforcement on the ground of the manner of application of the new test in the case. Local 23, AFM v. NLRB,

12 F.4th 778 (D.C. Cir. 2021). The court allowed that the Board may wish to proceed with the test afresh or "develop a new test altogether."

Page 140. Add after carryover paragraph before section break:

On April 4, 2022, General Counsel Abruzzo issued Memorandum GC 22–04, arguing that the Board should reconsider case precedent dating back to *Babcock & Wilcox Co.*, 77 NLRB 577 (1948), that has tolerated mandatory meetings in which employees are forced to listen to employer speech concerning the exercise of their statutory labor rights, especially during organizing campaigns. She contended that these "captive audience" meetings inherently involve an explicit or implicit unlawful threat that employees will be disciplined or suffer other reprisals if they exercise their protected right not to listen to such speech. Thus, according to the Memorandum, such meetings are a license to coerce and thereby an anomaly in labor law inconsistent with the Act's protection of employees' free choice and based on a fundamental misunderstanding of employers' speech rights. Thus, the General Counsel announced her intention to urge that mandatory meetings in which employees are forced to convene on paid time or are cornered by management while performing their job duties are unlawful. General Counsel Memos are available here: https://www.nlrb.gov/guidance/memos-research/general-counsel-memos.

On April 11, 2022, General Counsel included this argument before the Board in a brief in support of exceptions in *CEMEX Construction Materials Pacific LLC*, 28–CA–230115. To strike a balance between employees' Section 7 rights not to listen and an employer's Section 8(c) free speech right to express views, argument, or opinion concerning Section 7 activity, counsel proposed prophylactic safeguards are necessary to neutralize the implicit threat of reprisal in captive audience meetings. These proposed safeguards are as follows:

> **Convened Employees.** If an employer convenes employees for a Section 7 meeting on paid time, it must satisfy the following requirements to make the meeting voluntary. First, the employer must explain the purpose of the meeting. Second, the employer must assure employees:
>
> a. that attendance is voluntary,
>
> b. that if they attend, they will be free to leave at any time,
>
> c. that nonattendance will not result in reprisals (including loss of pay if the meeting occurs during their regularly scheduled working hours), and
>
> d. that attendance will not result in rewards or benefits.
>
> If an employer announces a meeting in advance, it must reiterate the explanation and assurances set forth above at the start of the meeting. Finally, the meeting must occur in a

context free from employer hostility to the exercise of Section 7 rights.

Cornered Employees. If an employer corners employees to address them concerning their exercise of Section 7 rights, it must satisfy the following requirements to ensure that the meeting is voluntary. First, the employer must explain the purpose of the encounter. Second, the employer must assure employees:

a. that participation is voluntary,

b. that nonparticipation will not result in reprisals (including loss of pay), and

c. that participation will not result in rewards or benefits.

Furthermore, because employees cannot ordinarily choose to leave their work area, the employer must obtain affirmative consent to talk to the employees there and assure them that they may end the encounter at any time without loss of pay (either by leaving or by asking the employer to stop). Finally, the encounter must occur in a context free from employer hostility to the exercise of Section 7 rights.

The brief is available here: https://www.nlrb.gov/case/28-CA-230115.

Page 141. Add after the first paragraph of A Note on "Salting":

"Salting" had been a technique deployed primarily in the construction trades; at least, most of the cases arose in that sector. Recently, however, it has become a feature in organizational efforts in service industries such as Starbucks and Chipotle. Josh Eidelson, *Undercover Organizers Become Secret Force in Labor Union Wins*, BLOOMBERG NEWS (April 3, 2023).

Page 145. Add to the end of the first full paragraph:

On how to demonstrate discriminatory application of employer email policies under the approach set forth in *The Register-Guard*, see *Communications Workers v. NLRB*, 6 F.4th 15, (D.C. Cir. 2021) (finding the Board erred in relying on its own post hoc distinction between permissible and impermissible employee conduct to reject the evidence of disparate treatment).

Page 156. Add after *Caesars Entertainment*:

The Communication Workers Union was organizing the workers at a T-Mobile call center. A union supporter emailed her coworkers from her company email address encouraging them to join the union's organizational efforts. She wrote, "Feel free to contact me with any questions, but please do so outside of working hours." She was disciplined for it. A charge of unfair labor practice ensued. The General Counsel argued *inter alia* the Company's purported application of its no solicitation policies was applied discriminatorily. The Board found no unfair labor practice, applying *Caesars Entertainment's* analysis that wrongful discrimination could occur only when there was disparate treatment of communications "of a similar character because of [the communicator's] union or other section 7-protected status," and reiterating the proposition in *Register Guard* that discrimination would be found if the employer allowed anti-union communications, but not pro-union ones. T-Mobile USA, Inc., 369 NLRB No. 90 (2020).

The District of Columbia Circuit disagreed, noting its rejection of that approach in *Register Guard* itself. Communications Workers v. NLRB, 6 F.4th 15 (D.C. Cir. 2021). The court stated that, in this case, as there, the Company's policies did not draw the distinction the Board applied:

> [T]he consistency of an employer's responses to union-related and nonunion employee conduct is measured not by whether the employer or Board can identify a legitimate, union-neutral distinction after the fact that the employer might lawfully have drawn, but by reference to the policies the employer actually had in place and the reasons on which it in fact relied for the action challenged as discriminatory. Because *Guard Publishing* itself, like this case, involved use of company email, speculation as to whether the Board might apply a different standard in cases not involving "the use of employer equipment" is of no moment here.

In *T-Mobile USA, Inc.,* 371 NLRB No. 163 (2022), the Board unanimously accepted as the law of the case the court's conclusion that the Respondent engaged in discrimination within the meaning of Register Guard. The Board's majority, consisting of Members Kaplan and Ring, found it unnecessary to address the General Counsel's invitation to revisit *Register Guard*'s discrimination standard. Member Prouty dissented from this declination.

Page 161. In the note on *Wyman-Gordon* at the bottom of the page, replace the second sentence (beginning with "The Wyman. . .) with the following two sentences:

The Wyman-Gordon Company refused to provide the names and addresses of company employees after the Board ordered a representation election, and refused as well to comply with a subpoena issued by the Board for the names and addresses. The Court of Appeals for the First Circuit held that the *Excelsior* requirement was a "rule" as defined by the Administrative Procedure Act (i.e., "an agency statement of general or particular applicability and future effect") and that the Board had therefore not promulgated it through proper procedures when it formulated the "rule" in the context of an "adjudication" concerning the validity of the Excelsior election.

2. ELECTION PROPAGANDA

(a) *Threats of Reprisal*

Page 169. Add at end of Problem for Discussion carried over from prior page:

1. After the Amazon Labor Union (ALU) won a representation election at an Amazon warehouse on Staten Island, the Company filed twenty-five objections to the election. Amazon.com Services LLC's Objections to the Results of the Election, NLRB Case No. 29–RC–288020 (April 8, 2022). Many of the objections alleged a breach of neutrality by Board agents; but some concerned ALU's conduct. During its anti-union campaign, the Company made extensive use of captive audience meetings. *See* Noam Scheiber, *Mandatory Meetings at Amazon Reveal its Approach to Resisting Unions*, *N.Y. Times*, March 25, 2022 at p. B1. As the *Times'* report noted: "The company has required employees to attend anti-labor sessions—typically, more than 20 per day. . . ." Amazon's Objection 15 alleged a course of union action that it claims to have upset the conditions required for a fair election:

> The ALU engaged in repeated and deliberate attempts to interfere with and "shut down" Amazon's small group meetings, solicited employees during Amazon's educational meetings in violation of Amazon's policies, and destroyed Amazon's campaign materials. The ALU's actions intentionally created hostile confrontations in front of eligible voters and hindered Amazon's lawful right to communicate its views to employees during the campaign. *See, e.g., Livingston Shirt Corp.*, 107 NLRB 400, 406–07, 409 (1953) (union has no right to campaign or solicit during employer's lawful small group meetings); *United Steelworkers of Am. v. NLRB*, 646 F.2d 616, 627 (D.C. Cir. 1981) (same, unless an employer has a broad rule prohibiting solicitation during nonworking time [Amazon has no such policy]).

Assume for the sake of analysis that the factual allegations are accurate. Under current law should the election be set aside?

2. A small conservative political publication has a staff of seven editorial writers. The owner maintains a Twitter account followed by several thousand. After another media outlet unionized he posted a tweet, "FYI" his publication, "first one of you tries to unionize I swear I'll send you back to the salt mine." No editorial writer complained; but one of the tweet's readers filed a charge of unfair labor practice. Has the owner committed an unfair labor practice? FDRLST Media, LLC v. NLRB, 35 F.4th 108 (3rd Cir. 2022).

Page 174. Add after Problem 3:

Amazon CEO, Andy Jessy, was interviewed in connection with the effort by the American Labor Union to unionize the workers at an Amazon warehouse in Staten Island, New York. He responded to a question on CNBC that if a union were selected

(a) employees would be less empowered in the workplace;

(b) it would be more difficult for employees to have direct relationships with management; and

(c) things would be done less quickly and more bureaucratically.

And to an interviewer on Bloomberg that

(a) employees are better off without a union;

(b) it would be more difficult for employees to have direct relationships with their managers if employees were represented by a union; and

(c) it would be more bureaucratic and difficult to get things done quickly if employees were represented by a union.

The American Labor Union filed a charge of violation of § 8(a)(1). The Regional Director has filed a Complaint: Amazon.com Services LLC, Case No. 10-CA-297441 (Oct. 25, 2022). In light of Section 8(c), should the complaint have been issued? *Cf.* Tesla, Inc. v. NLRB, 65 F.4th 981 (5th Cir. 2023). (Elon Musk tweets, "Nothing stopping Tesla team at our car plant from voting union. Could do so tmrw if they wanted. But why pay union dues & give up stock options for nothing?").

3. OTHER FORMS OF INTERFERENCE, RESTRAINT OR COERCION

Page 196. Add after the carryover paragraph, above Problems for Discussion:

An employer may engage in coercive interrogation into non-protected activity. But what of the non-protected activity—a strike in violation of a no-strike provision in a collective bargaining agreement—that is intertwined with protected protest? The Board had adopted a two-pronged requirement: that the questioning must "focus closely" on the unprotested activity; and must intrude only "minimally" into protected activity. The Second Circuit affirmed the first limb, but remanded the second. Time Warner Cable v. NLRB, 982 F.3d 127 (2d Cir. 2020).

A recurring scenario involves an employer's interrogation of employees in preparing for Board unfair labor practice proceedings. On the one hand, the Board has long recognized that coercion can be present in any interrogation of employees involving union activity. On the other hand, an employer has a right to mount a full defense. The Board struck balance in a "bright time" rule, akin to the *Strucknes* rule, in *Johnnie's Poultry*, 146 NLRB 770 (1964) *enf. den.* 344 F.2d 617 (6th Cir. 1965):

> [T]he employer must communicate to the employee the purpose of the questioning, assure him that no reprisal will take place, and obtain his participation on a voluntary basis; the questioning must occur in a context free from employer hostility to union organization and must not be itself coercive in nature; and the questions must not exceed the necessities of the legitimate purpose by prying into other union matters, eliciting information concerning an employee's subjective state of mind, or otherwise interfering with the statutory rights of employees.

Most courts of appeals have affirmed the bright line approach; but some have not, in favor of a "totality of the circumstances" test. *See* Sunbelt Rentals, Inc., 372 NLRB No. 24 (2022) (slip. op. n. 8 noting the judicial record). After inviting amicus briefs in *Sunbelt Rentals*, the Board, by a 3 to 2 vote and in a set of lengthy opinions on both sides, affirmed its adherence to *Johnnie's Poultry*. In the case two employees were interviewed by the company's lawyer in preparation for an unfair labor practice hearing. One was not told that his answers would not affect his job; the other was not told that participation in the interview was voluntary.

B. COMPANY DOMINATION OR ASSISTANCE

Page 216. Add after *Electromation*, above Problems for Discussion:

The District of Columbia Circuit recently remanded to the Board to clarify what group activity ("dealing") was requisite to render an employee participation group a labor organization. Communications Workers v. NLRB, 994 F.3d 653 (D.C. Cir. 2021). On remand, the Board, in a 2–1 decision, held the company's "T-Voice" to be a labor organization. (Because the company created it, dominance was not contested.) Under T-Voice the company selected "representatives" from customer service centers to channel complaints and questions from customers and from call center employees dealing with the quality of service. Some of these questions dealt with or bore upon compensation and working conditions. Management informed the relevant representative when it acted on some of these complaints. The Board had earlier held that absent evidence that these complaints were generated by a group there was no "dealing" within the meaning of section 2(5). On remand, the Board held that proposals made to management by T-Value employee representatives *as* T-Voice employee representatives constituted group proposals; and as these were considered and acted on by management—to accept or reject, by word or deed—there was a course of "dealing" under the Act.

C. DISCRIMINATION

Page 231. In the first sentence under the heading THE "DISCRIMINATION" REQUIREMENT, replace *Mueller Brass* with *Nichols Aluminum*.

Page 247. Add after the first paragraph of Problem 2:

On the showing of animus necessary under *Wright Line*, see *Cordura Restaurants, Inc. v. NLRB*, 985 F.3d 415 (5th Cir. 2021). On the showing of animus where an entire group, not only union supporters, is discharged, see *Napleton 1050, Inc. v. NLRB*, 976 F.3d (D.C. Cir. 2020).

Page 261. Add to end of Problem 2:

Under the Age Discrimination in Employment Act (ADEA) a worker asserting age discrimination can make out a prima facie violation by showing that he was over age 65, was qualified to do the job, was discharged, and a substantially younger person placed in his position. At that point the burden shifts to the employer to provide evidence of a "legitimate non-discriminatory reason" for the discharge.

Gene Kelly was a 50 year old "group leader," a supervisor, at Tackett Auto Parts Mfg., Inc. Kelly was terminated and a 30 year old employee from another group was transferred to and made group leader for Kelly's group. Kelly has sued under the ADEA. Tackett has moved for summary judgment. It argues that as a union was seeking to organize the workforce it made clear to all group leaders that "they were expected to convince their supervisees not to support the union," that Kelly had been repeatedly told that he was not taking "sufficient steps to lead his group to believe they did not need a union," and that after management saw that Kelly's team had the largest number of employees in any group wearing union t-shirts he was dismissed for "lack of strong leadership". Should Tackett's motion be granted? Keller v. Hyundai Motor Mfg., 513 F.Supp.3d 1324 (M.D. Ala. 2021). *Cf.* Karen Weise & Noam Scheiber, *Amazon Managers Fired In Wake of Union Victory*, N.Y. Times (May 7, 2022), p. B1.

D. REMEDIES FOR UNFAIR LABOR PRACTICES

Page 270. Add at the end of Question 1:

In its settlement agreement with the Board, Amazon has agreed to post the agreed upon notice at all of its fulfillment, sortation, and receive) centers, as well as delivery stations, nationwide. The agreement is available here: https://foiaonline.gov/foiaonline/action/public/submissionDetails?tracking Number=NLRB-2022-000336&type=Request.

Page 271. Add at end of Question 2:

Camelot Terrace was glossed by the District of Columbia Circuit in *NLRB v. Ampersand Publishing, LLC*, 43 F.4th 1233 (D.C. Cir. 2022). The court stated that the Board lacks the power to order attorney fees as a *litigation* expense, not for expenses incurred in collective bargaining where an employer has bargained in bad faith. The two were segregable.

II. SELECTION OF THE REPRESENTATIVE FOR THE PURPOSES OF COLLECTIVE BARGAINING

A. GROUNDS FOR NOT PROCEEDING TO AN INVESTIGATION AND CERTIFICATION

Page 276. Insert after the last full paragraph:

In *Rieth-Riley Construction Co., Inc.*, 371 NLRB No. 109 (2022), the Board held that this rule continues to permit merit-determination dismissals of election petitions, distinguishing these dismissals from those charges covered by the rule's changes to the blocking-charge policy. Merit-determination dismissals are reserved for a narrow subset of egregious ULP charges that, if proven, require dismissal of the petition, and they hinge on a determination by a Regional Director that the charge has merit (instead of resting on the mere pendency of a charge).

On November 4, 2022, the Biden Board published a purposed rule for representation case procedures, entitled the Fair Choice and Employee Voice Rule. Issued in a 3–2 vote, this proposed rule would unwind portions of the April 2020 Rule addressing election-blocking charges, voluntary recognition, and construction industry bargaining relationships. *See* 87 FR 66890 (November 4, 2022).

According to the majority, the rule is designed to restore the Board's prior law in these three areas and would better protect workers' ability to make a free choice regarding representation, as well as promote stability in labor relations and encourage collective bargaining. Specifically, the rule would amend the April 2020 Final Rule in the following three ways:

1) The rule would return to the Board's long-established blocking charge policy as most recently reflected in a 2014 rule. Under that approach, when unfair labor practice charges are filed while an election petition is pending, a Regional Director may delay the election if the conduct alleged threatens to interfere with employee free choice.
2) The rule would eliminate the required notice-and-election procedure triggered by an employer's voluntary recognition of a union based on a showing of majority support among employees.
3) The rule would return to the Board's prior approach to voluntary recognition in the construction industry, as reflected in its case law. This would include restoring a six-month limitations period for election petitions challenging a construction employer's voluntary recognition of a union under Section 9(a) of the Act. It would also include the principle (established in *Staunton Fuel*) that sufficiently detailed language in a collective-bargaining agreement can serve as sufficient evidence that voluntary recognition was based on Section 9(a) of the Act.

Following its initial publication, the Board twice extended the deadline for comments, with the last date for the comment period being March 1, 2023. As of the date of this Supplement, no final rule has been issued.

Page 278. Add after the carryover paragraph:

In *Mountaire Farms, Inc.*, 370 NLRB No. 110 (2021), the Board decided not to modify the contract bar doctrine.

B. APPROPRIATE BARGAINING UNIT

2. CRITERIA FOR UNIT DETERMINATIONS

Page 288. Add after discussion of *PCC Structurals*:

By a 3 to 2 vote, the Board overruled *PCC Structurals* and reinstated *Specialty Healthcare*. American Steel Construction, Inc., 372 NLRB No. 23 (2022). Both the majority and dissenting opinions are lengthy: the majority reasoned that it was adhering both to longstanding precedent and to the policy of the Act, opining that the "overwhelming community of interest" standard was merely a shorthand way of phrasing the established principle. The dissent contested the majority's characterization and stressed the failure to address the interests of those who would not be included in the petitioned-for unit. The majority took strong objection to the interests of those not petitioned-for having any bearing on whether the petitioned-for unit was "an" appropriate one.

Page 289. Add after the carryover paragraph:

The Machinists Union petitioned for a unit of 87 tool and die makers at Nissan Motors in Tennessee. The Regional Director ordered an election for the "wall-to-wall" unit of all 4,300 workers at the plant which the Union did not seek to represent. The decision has been appealed to the Board. BLOOMBERG LAW NEWS (June 14, 2021).

4. MULTIEMPLOYER AND COORDINATED BARGAINING

Page 305. Add at end of first full paragraph:

The court later held that the Board's initial decision in *Browning-Ferris* continued to apply to the company. Sanitary Truck Drivers and Helpers Local 305 v. NLRB, 45 F.4th 38 (D.C. Cir. 2022).

Page 307. Add at end of text:

On December 10, 2021, the Labor Board posted a notice that it will "engage in rulemaking on the standard for determining whether two employers. . .are a joint employer under the Act."

III. SECURING BARGAINING RIGHTS THROUGH UNFAIR LABOR PRACTICE PROCEEDINGS

Page 343. Add to the end of Problem 2:

On April 11, 2022, in a brief in *CEMEX Construction Materials Pacific LLC*, 28–CA–230115, General Counsel indeed has now urged the Board to reinstate the *Joy Silk* doctrine (discussed in *Gissel* on page 327). Counsel argued that the Board should return to the *Joy Silk* because the current remedial scheme (under *Gissel* and *Linden Lumber*) has failed to deter unfair labor practices during union organizing drives and provide for free and fair elections. The *Joy Silk* approach would cure this problem, because, once the union has collected enough cards to show majority support, the burden would be on the employer to show a "good faith doubt" as to the union's majority status in order to refuse to bargain, and the employer would not be able to demonstrate this if it has engaged in unfair labor practices. Counsel further argued that the Board retains the authority to reinstate the doctrine given the substantial deference it enjoys in enacting national labor policy; the doctrine is rational and consistent with the Act, and it strikes an appropriate balance between employees' Section 7 rights to choose whether or not to select union representation. In light of what you have learned so far about representation elections and potential employer unfair labor practices, should the Board do so? The briefs in *CEMEX* can be found here: https://www.nlrb.gov/case/28-CA-230115.

The General Counsel renewed this request in *ArrMaz Products, Inc.*, 372 NLRB No. 12 (2022). However, the Board held that the case, which was heard on a motion for summary judgment, was not a suitable vehicle to reconsider *Ex-Cello*. Member Ring addressed *Ex-Cello* on the merits.

Page 361. Add to Problems for Discussion:

6. A union was certified as the bargaining representative on January 15. After the expiration of the certification year no contract had been made. A statement was then signed by 8 of the bargaining unit's 10 employees and given to the employee stating: "we disagree with bringing the union in." The statement was not supported by the Employer, which promptly withdrew recognition. Was the withdrawal a violation of Section 8(a)(5)? Hampton Inn-Long Island Brookhaven, 371 NLRB No. 103 (2022).

be or she might be able to show good faith doubt as to the union's majority [illegible] in order to refuse to bargain, and the employer would not be able to demonstrate that it has engaged in unfair labor practices. Counsel for the [illegible] argued that the Board retains the authority to reinstate the doctrine given [illegible] interests it enjoys in enacting national labor policy, the doctrine is rational and consistent with the Act, and it strikes an appropriate balance between employees' freedom of choice to choose whether or not to select union representation. In light of what you have learned so far about [illegible] elections and potential employer unfair labor practices, [illegible] the Board do? The brief in [illegible] can be found here: [illegible] 2501 [illegible].

[illegible] reconsider Joy Silk [illegible] Cemex [illegible]

Page 301. Add to Problems for Discussion:

[illegible] union was certified as the bargaining representative on January 1. After the expiration of the certification year no contract had been made. A statement was then signed by 8 of the bargaining unit's 10 employees and given to the employer stating, "We disagree with bringing the union in." The statement was not authored by the employer, which promptly withdrew recognition. Was the withdrawal a violation of Section 8(a)(5)? [illegible] Long Island Brookhaven, 371 NLRB No. 105 (2022).

PART THREE

NEGOTIATION OF THE COLLECTIVE BARGAINING AGREEMENT

I. EXCLUSIVE REPRESENTATION AND MAJORITY RULE

Page 378. Add at the end of Problem 1:

While a union is bargaining for a collective agreement a group of employees walk out because they believe that new hires are being paid at a higher rate than more senior workers. They are discharged. Has the employer committed an unfair labor practice? NLRB v. Noah's Ark Processors, LLC, 31 F.4th 1097 (8th Cir. 2022).

II. THE DUTY TO BARGAIN IN GOOD FAITH

Page 404. Add to the end of Problem 1:

Crozer-Chester Med. Center v. NLRB, 976 F.3d 276 (3rd Cir. 2020) (on whether an employer's entire Asset Purchase Agreement must be disclosed).

Page 425. Add after the second full paragraph:

In *Stericycle, Inc.*, 170 NLRB No. 89 (2021), the Republican majority held Section 8(a)(5) was not violated by the Company's unilateral distribution of an employee handbook to all employees, unionized and not, that set out terms and conditions of employment that differed at points from the provisions of the collective bargaining agreement governing its unionized employees but that recited without more that "in some cases these policies may be impacted by collective bargaining agreements."

V. BARGAINING REMEDIES

Page 511. Add to the end of the discussion of *Tidee* and *Ex-Cell-O*:

General Counsel Abruzzo has issued two memoranda expanding on the remedies that office intends to seek in order to achieve greater "make whole" relief. GC Mem. 21–06 and 21–07 (2021). The Labor Board followed up in *Thryv, Inc.*, 372 NLRB No. 22 (2022). By vote of 3 to 2, in lengthy opinions for the majority and the dissent, the Board held that all cases in which "make whole" relief will be ordered the relief should include "all direct or foreseeable pecuniary harms" the affected employees had endured as a result of the respondent's unfair labor practice. (Italics in original.) It strove to explain that those remedies—medical insurance costs, damage to clothing, legal expenses, damage to property, and a good deal more—noting of prior decisions where these were ordered that these were not "consequential damages" as that is understood in tort law and raised no problem under the Seventh Amendment. The dissent did not dispute that the Board's power to order "make whole" relief extended to more than back pay, but opined the approach the majority charted was "overbroad."

Building on the *Thryv* decision, in *Noah's Ark Processors, LLC*, 372 NLRB No. 80 (2023), the Board detailed potential remedies it will consider when employers have shown repeated or egregious disregard for employees' rights under the Act. The Board determined that when the unfair labor practice violations found in a case justify a "broad" cease-and-desist order, which is traditionally ordered in cases where the Respondent has shown a proclivity to violate the Act or has engaged in egregious or widespread misconduct, the Board should consider (in addition to the cease-and-desist order) and apply some or all of a non-exhaustive list of potential remedies. Such remedies may include:

- Adding an Explanation of Rights to the remedial order that informs employees of their rights in a more comprehensive manner;
- Requiring a reading and distribution of the Notice and any Explanation of Rights to employees, including potentially requiring supervisors or particular officials involved in the violations to participate in or be present for the reading and/or allowing presence of a union agent during the reading;
- Mailing the Notice and any Explanation of Rights to the employees' homes;
- Requiring a person who bears significant responsibility in the Respondent's organization to sign the Notice;
- Publication of the Notice in local publications of broad circulation and local appeal;
- Requiring that the Notice/Explanation be posted for an extended period of time;
- Visitation requirement, permitting representatives of the Board to inspect the Respondent's bulletin boards and records to determine and secure compliance with the Board's order;
- Reimbursement of Union's bargaining expenses, including making whole any employees who lost wages by attending bargaining sessions.

Over the dissent of Member Kaplan, the two-member majority emphasized that providing this guidance will enhance consistency in the exercise of the Board's discretion, and the consideration and implementation of the full range of appropriate remedies.

In *Noah's Ark Processors* itself, the Board therefore upheld the ALJ's finding that the employer repeatedly bargained in bad faith with the union, but then added that the employer's hostility toward its responsibilities under Act warranted further remedies. In addition to traditional remedies for refusal to bargain, the Board ordered variations on many of the items listed above, including robust notice, visitation, and expense reimbursement remedies. See also NLRB v. Neises Corp., 62 F.4th 1040 (7th Cir. 2023), on extensive contempt remedies for persistent refusals to bargain.

In [illegible] NLRB [illegible] the Board [illegible] upheld the ALJ's finding that the employer repeatedly bargained in bad faith with the union, but then added that the employer's [illegible] toward its responsibilities under the Act warranted further remedies. In addition to traditional remedies for refusal to bargain, the Board ordered variations on many of the items listed above, including reading notice, visitation, and expense reimbursement [illegible] remedies. See also NLRB v. [illegible] [illegible] extraordinary remedies for persistent refusals to bargain.

PART FOUR

PROTESTS AND PICKETING, STRIKES AND BOYCOTTS

I. RIGHTS OF EMPLOYEE PROTESTERS UNDER THE NLRA

A. PROTECTED AND UNPROTECTED CONCERTED ACTIVITY

Page 535. Add to Questions for Discussion:

5. Betsy Ross is an activities coordinator in rehabilitative services at Memorial Hospital in Lower Lothian (MHLL). The hospital's nursing staff is unionized; the other staff members including Ms. Ross are not. MHLL has been acquired by Middle American Healthcare (MAH). In the months after the acquisition, the nurses' union petitioned hospital management complaining about a reduction in nursing staff, claiming overwork and a lack of patient care, and demanding a return to the prior staffing level. The local newspaper, the *Lower Lothian Intelligencer*, has given extensive coverage to the dispute.

Ms. Ross submitted a letter to the editor of the *Intelligencer*. In her letter, she referenced previous newspaper articles and expressed support for the nurses in their dispute. She applauded the nurses for submitting their petition, urged management to heed the nurses' staffing demands, and opined that they were rightly concerned about risks to patient safety posed by understaffing. She also criticized management as unduly allegiant to MAH and out of touch with patient care, arguing that these shortcomings negatively affected hospital staff and the local community. Young did not discuss her letter with any other employee prior to submitting it.

Ms. Ross has been given a five-day suspension without pay for "a grievous act of disloyalty to MHLL tending to tarnish its image in the community and to disparage the quality of patient care." Has MHLL violated Section 8(a)(1) of the Labor Act? NLRB v. Maine Coast Regional Health Facilities, 999 F.3d 1 (1st Cir. 2021).

6. Sean O'Hara drives a truck for the County Cork Concrete Company (CCCC), a non-unionized enterprise. Kevin O'Flaherty is the terminal manager. There are six other drivers at that location. O'Flaherty gave O'Hara a $3/hr. raise but told him "to tell no one else. That's a strict company policy." O'Hara told his assistant, Michael Flinn, who'd only gotten a $1.50/hr. raise. Flinn was furious and told the other drivers who'd gotten that same amount. They went as a group to O'Flaherty and threatened to quit if they were not given a $3/hr. raise. O'Flaherty called in O'Hara, told him he was fired "for breach of company policy and for 'causing a mutiny'." Has CCCC committed an unfair labor practice? Morgan Corp., 371 NLRB No. 142 (2022).

Page 536. Add to Problems for Discussion:

3. Does a permanent strike placement enjoy *Weingarten* rights? Troy Grove, 371 NLRB No. 138 (2022).

Page 555. Under the heading "III," replace the second sentence with the following three sentences:

Even if the Arbitration Act normally requires us to enforce arbitration agreements like theirs, the employees reply that the NLRA overrides that guidance in these cases and commands us to hold their agreements unlawful yet. This argument faces a stout uphill climb. When confronted with two Acts of Congress allegedly touching on the same topic, this Court is not at "liberty to pick and choose among congressional enactments" and must instead strive " 'to give effect to both.' "

Page 584. Add after the first full paragraph:

In *Dish Network, LLC,* 370 NLRB No. 97 (2021), the Board reaffirmed the validity of required confidentiality attached to arbitrations conducted under Company policies in application to hearings, discovery, and awards. However, "settlements" were held not to be swept into the Federal Arbitration Act and requiring confidentiality on that violated the Labor Act.

Page 589. Add at the end of the carryover paragraph:

Moreover, in *Glacier Northwest, Inc. v. International Brotherhood of Teamsters,* 143 S. Ct. 1404 (2023) (reproduced in Part VIII of this Supplement), the Supreme Court held 8–1 that striking union drivers of the employer's ready-mix concrete delivery trucks did not take reasonable precautions to protect employer's property from imminent danger resulting from the drivers' sudden cessation of work while trucks were full of concrete, and thus, the Act did not "arguably protect" the union's conduct or preempt the employer's state law tort claims against the union.

Page 598. Add to Problems for Discussion:

8. The workers at Kellogg's Nabisco plants have been on strike at four locations nationally. They voted overwhelming to reject the collective agreement the union's leadership had negotiated and to continue the strike. Nabisco announced it was accepting applications for permanent strike replacements. A posting on Reddit encouraged readers to clog Kellogg's application process by pretending to be a local resident applying for the job and provided a link on which applications could be made. According to a press account, almost 60,000 such applications have been made. Assuming that it would be possible to connect the union to the Reddit posting, would it have committed any unfair labor practice?

Page 605. Add after General Motors:

In *Lion Elastomers LLC*, 372 NLRB No. 83 (2023), the Biden Board overturned the Trump Board's decision in *General Motors*, returning to the "setting-specific" standards approach applicable in situations in which employees are disciplined or discharged for misconduct that occurs during activity otherwise protected by Section 7. The decision was 3–1, with Member Kaplan dissenting.

Noting that labor disputes are often heated, the Board reaffirmed the principle that, to safeguard their Section 7 rights, employees must be given some leeway while engaging in protected concerted activity. Thus, contrary to approach adopted in *General Motors*, the Board held that employee conduct while engaging in such important activity must be treated differently than if it had occurred in an ordinary workplace context.

The Board emphasized that no federal court has ever rejected any of the three setting-specific standards. They are: (1) the *Atlantic Steel* test, which governs employees' conduct towards management in the workplace; (2) the totality-of-the-circumstances test, which governs social media posts and most cases involving conversations among employees in the workplace; and (3) the *Clear Pine Mouldings* standard, which governs picket-line conduct.

The Board also rejected as unpersuasive the other reasons offered in General Motors for abandoning the setting-specific standards approach, including the claim that this approach leads to unpredictable results. Perhaps most notably, the Board detailed why this approach does not conflict with federal antidiscrimination law:

> Nor is the claim that the setting-specific standards inherently tend to impose legal obligations on employers that conflict with their obligations under antidiscrimination laws well founded. It is certainly true that in administering the Act, the Board must accommodate other Federal statutes insofar as they apply, just as other Federal statutes must accommodate the Act. But the General Motors Board cited no judicial decisions finding an actual conflict between an employer's duties under the Act and its duties under Federal antidiscrimination law. Indeed, the General Motors Board cited no cases brought under antidiscrimination law where an employer was even alleged to have violated the law by complying with its obligation under the Act not to discharge or discipline an employee who had committed misconduct in the course of protected activity.
>
> The case law contradicts the view of the *General Motors* Board. A good example is the Eighth Circuit's picket-line misconduct decision in *Cooper Tire & Rubber Co. v. NLRB*, 866

F.3d 885 (8th Cir. 2017), a case the General Motors Board simply ignored. In *Cooper Tire & Rubber*, the court enforced the Board's order requiring reinstatement of a striker who had directed racist taunts at a van carrying replacement workers that had just crossed the picket line. It agreed with the Board's application of the *Clear Pine Mouldings* standard and rejected the employer's argument that *Wright Line* should apply. 866 F.3d at 889–890. It also rejected the argument that the Board's order conflicted with the employer's duty under Title VII, 42 U.S.C. §§ 2000e, et seq. *Id.* at 891- 892. The court explained that the striker's picket-line jibes—racially offensive, stereotyped comments about food—did not create a hostile work environment, nor did Title VII create any legal obligation to fire the striker. *Id.* at 892.

The Eighth Circuit's decision is not anomalous. The Supreme Court has said repeatedly that Title VII is not "a general civility code for the American workplace." As the Court has explained, "offhand comments and isolated incidents (unless extremely serious) will not amount to discriminatory changes in the terms and conditions of employment." There is no obvious or inevitable conflict, then, between the Board's approach as reflected in the setting-specific standards and Federal antidiscrimination law. The *General Motors* Board cited no judicial support for the proposition that employers have a legal duty under antidiscrimination law to discipline or discharge employees in every instance involving the sort of "offhand comments and isolated incidents"—those that are not "extremely serious"—which the Board typically would find retained the protection of the Act if they occurred in the course of Section 7 activity.

As you turn to the *Questions for Discussion* below, consider them in light of both the *General Motors* decision and the Board's response in *Lion Elastomers*.

Page 606. Add after Questions for Discussion:

On remand, *Constellium Rolled Pdts., LLC*, 371 NLRB No. 16 (2021), the Board reaffirmed its decision that the General Counsel had satisfied his initial burden under *Wright Line*, reiterating that animus "may be established by circumstantial evidence." Analysis accordingly turned to the Company's argument that the discharge was motivated by its efforts to comply with antidiscrimination law. The Board rejected the claim. The Company permitted the common use of the term "whore board" in its workplace to refer to the overtime signup sheets. The Respondent's lack of enforcement of its obligations under antidiscrimination laws allowing wide use of the term persisted for some 6 months, until Williams [the employee] alone was singled out for discipline and discharge for use of the term. The District of Columbia Circuit enforced the Board's order under *Wright Line*. Constellation Rolled Pdts., LLC v. NLRB, 45 F.4th 234 (D.C. Cir. 2022).

II. CONSTITUTIONAL LIMITATIONS ON GOVERNMENT REGULATION

B. PICKETING AND FREEDOM OF COMMUNICATION

Page 684. Add following the photograph and before Problem for Discussion:

In *Lippert Components, Inc.*, 371 NLRB No. 8 (2021), the Board affirmed the ALJ's application of *Eliason & Knuth*. Chairman McFerran did so on the ground of *Elias & Knuth's* conformity with the Act; Members Kaplan and Ring on first amendment grounds. Member Emmanuel dissented.

III. THE NATIONAL LABOR RELATIONS ACT

B. SECONDARY PRESSURE

1. UNDER THE TAFT-HARTLEY ACT

Page 723. Add at end of Problem 8:

CP Anchorage Hotel 2, LLC v. Unite Here! Local 878, 558 F. Supp. 3d 800 (D. Alaska 2021).

Page 725. Add after *Moore Dry Dock* above Problems for Discussion:

On *Moore Dry Dock*, see *SEIU Local 87 v. NLRB*, 995 F.3d 1032 (9th Cir. 2021).

---

2. THE 1959 AMENDMENTS: CONSUMER APPEALS

Page 746. Add at end of Problem for Discussion:

2. The union representing the workers at Nabisco, producers of Oreo cookies, is on strike. Assume that a union agent has been stationed at the customer entrance of the Pioneer Food Market to hand out handbills urging customers not to buy Nabisco products. Pioneer is not unionized. Pioneer retail clerk Delphine Katz was restocking the store's shelf of Oreo cookies when a customer, who'd been given a handbill at the entrance, gave the handbill to Katz. Katz placed an adhesive backing on the handbill and attached it to the Oreo display placard on the store's shelf, shown below. A store manager saw her do it. He photographed what she had done—shown below—and sent it to the corporation's human resources department. If Ms. Katz is discharged would that be an unfair labor practice? Assume, instead, that on her break time Ms. Katz stationed herself in front of the Oreo display holding the handbill up for customers to see. She was told to cease the display or move away and she declined. Would her discharge for that be an unfair labor practice?

[Thanks to Professor Steve Willborn for bringing this photograph to our attention.]

C. VIOLENCE AND UNION RESPONSIBILITY

Page 775. Add at the end of the Problem for Discussion:

For the elements of union liability under the Racketeer Influenced and Corruption Act (RICO) for sabotage and extortion in the course of bitter labor dispute, see *Care One Management LLC v. United Healthcare Workers East*, 43 F.4th 126 (3rd Cir. 2022) and *Care One Management, LCC v. United Healthcare Workers East*, 22 F.4th 128 (3rd Cir. 2021).

PART FIVE

ADMINISTRATION OF THE COLLECTIVE AGREEMENT

III. JUDICIAL ENFORCEMENT OF COLLECTIVE AGREEMENTS

Page 809. Add at end of Problem 4:

Local 97, IBEW v. Niagara Mohawk Power Corp., 67 F.4th 107 (2d Cir. 2023) (softening the court's categorical distinction between "broad" and "narrow" arbitration clauses).

5. The Grievance Procedure in the collective bargaining agreement between Lupken Valve, LLC and the Metal Fabricators Union Local 51 provides in pertinent part:

> A grievance within the meaning of this agreement involves and is limited to the interpretation and application of any specific provision of this Agreement. Changes in business practice, matters involving capital expenditures. . .or any dispute which either directly or indirectly involves the interpretation or application of plans covering pensions. . .shall not be arbitrable.

A portion of the Article XII on Benefits provided for a "Company § 401(k) Plan" into which the Company would make matching contributions to the participating employees.

The Company informed the Union that it was temporarily reducing its matching 401(k) contribution by 50%. The Union has filed a grievance. The Company rejected it. The Union has filed notice of arbitration. The Company has moved in federal court for a declaratory judgment that the grievance is not arbitrable. How should the court rule? Johnson Controls Security Solutions, LLC v. Int'l Broth. of Electrical Workers, 24 F.4th 87 (1st Cir. 2022).

Page 810. Add at the end of Problem for Discussion:

On August 26, 2007, the Union filed a grievance for the failure to pay employees at the contractual overtime rate. Failing resolution the Union filed for arbitration. For unexplained reasons, the arbitration did not take place until June 12, 2013. At that time the Company asserted that the assignment of work hours was not within the scope of the grievance procedure and so the grievance was not substantively arbitrable. A hearing on the merits was suspended pending arbitration of the issue of substantive arbitrability. A year later the arbitrator held the claim to be arbitrable, but the Company sought judicial review of the award. In December, 2016, the courts sustained the arbitrator's decision. The hearing on the merits of the overtime claim began in 2018, wherein the Company asserted for the first time that the grievance was not timely as not having been filed within the contractually set period after knowledge of the claimed violation. The Union replied by pointing to one of the listing agency's rules that governed the proceeding: "a party that alleges a dispute is not arbitrable" must "include said claim in their submission". The Union argued that because no "said claim" was made by the Company at the time of its response to the grievance, the claim of timeliness it must be considered to have been waived. The arbitrator disagreed on the ground that the rule said "said claim," not all "said claims". The arbitrator held the grievance untimely. The Union has petitioned the court to set aside the decision and remand for a hearing on the merits. Both parties have moved for summary judgment. How should the court rule? Unión Internacional UAW v. Bacardi Corp., 8 F.4th 44 (1st Cir. 2021).

Page 823. Add at end of final paragraph:

Compare Monongahela Valley Hospital, cited in the text, *with Independent Laboratory Employees' Union v. Exxon Mobile Research & Engineering Co.*, 11 F.4th 210 (3rd Cir. 2021), enforcing an arbitration award on the basis of reliance on extrinsic evidence and the "common law of the shop".

Some courts have refused to enforce arbitral awards in discharge cases in which arbitrators have found the facts to evidence "cause" to dismiss, but who have reduced the discharge to lesser penalties in light of mitigating factors. These courts have reasoned that as "cause" has been found under the first part of the standard submission—"Was the grievant dismissed for just cause and, if not, what shall be the remedy?"—there is no more for the arbitrator. Are these cases faithful to *Enterprise Wheel*? Or is the matter merely how the award is drafted? W.M. Crittenden Operations, LLC v. United Food and Commercial Workers, 9 F.4th 732 (8th Cir. 2021).

Page 826. Add to Problems:

5. Art XV, § 1(g), of the parties' collective agreement sets out a "no fault attendance policy" providing for Progressive Discipline for up to four "occurrences" (defined as any absence within a twelve-month period) of warnings, suspension, and, on the fourth occurrence, discharge. A section of the Article on Grievances and Arbitration provides that "the only issue under this Article subject to [the Grievance-Arbitration provision] shall be whether the absence actually occurred." "Absence" is defined as any failure to report "dressed out and ready for work" at the exact time assigned. Art VII on Discharge provides that "no employee may be disciplined or discharged without just cause."

Able Nicht had three occurrences on his record. The Company's rules require employees to report "dressed and ready to work" at the beginning of their shifts; in Nicht's case, 7:00 am. Because he fumbled in donning his protective clothing, he clocked in for the mandatory safety meeting beginning the shift as dressed and ready to work at 7:02 am. He was discharged. The Union took his discharge to arbitration. The Arbitrator held that, under Art. VII, she had to consider all the circumstances of Mr. Nicht's conduct. She ordered Nicht to be reinstated and awarded less six months' pay (the case was heard fifteen months after the date of discharge). The Company has moved in federal court to vacate the award. The Union has moved to enforce it. How should the court rule? Warrior Met Coal Mining, LLC v. UMW, 28 F.4th 1073 (11th Cir. 2022).

IV. THE ROLE OF THE NATIONAL LABOR RELATIONS BOARD AND THE ARBITRATOR DURING THE TERM OF A COLLECTIVE AGREEMENT

A. CONDUCT WHICH ALLEGEDLY VIOLATES BOTH THE CONTRACT AND THE LABOR ACT

Page 879. Add at the end of the last paragraph on the page:

On the "clear and unmistakable" test, see *AC & S Inc. v. George*, 851 S.E.2d 495 (W. Va. 2020) (on the reach of a collective agreement to a retaliation claim under state law) and see *Wilson v. PBM, LLC*, 140 N.Y.S.3d 276 (App. Div. 2021) (on the substitution of labor arbitration for statutory discrimination claims).

B. THE DUTY TO BARGAIN DURING THE TERM OF AN EXISTING AGREEMENT

Page 916. Add to Problems for Discussion:

5. The Noyes Toys Company is unionized. Its collective agreement sets out a lengthy management rights clause that reserves to the Company the power to "issue all rules it deems necessary to achieve efficient and safe production and delivery of its products," that "all members of the bargaining unit will be bound to observe the terms of the Employee Handbook." The Handbook's section on drivers provides that, "In the event of any accident involving physical injury or damage in excess of $100 a check on the driver's driving history including any and all moving violations will be made."

The collective agreement expired on December 31. The parties are in the process of negotiating a new collective agreement. On January 3, the Company announced that, as of January 10, checks on driving history will be made annually for each driver. The Union has filed a charge of violation of Section 8(a)(5). The Company has responded that the change was consistent with its reservation of management rights. Should the General Counsel issue a complaint? NLRB v. Nexstar Broadcasting, Inc., 4 F.4th 801 (9th Cir. 2021).

[illegible] right to be reinstated and [illegible] less six or [illegible] part of a case were heard fifteen months after the date of discharge. The Company has moved in federal court to vacate the award. The Union has moved to enforce it. How should the court rule? [illegible] Coal Mining [illegible] (4th Cir. 2022).

IV. THE ROLE OF THE NATIONAL LABOR RELATIONS BOARD AND THE ARBITRATOR DURING THE TERM OF A COLLECTIVE AGREEMENT

[illegible]

Page [illegible]. Add at the end of the last paragraph on the page:

On the [illegible] and [illegible] [illegible] [illegible] (on the [illegible] of a collective agreement to a [illegible] claim under state law), and see [illegible] N.Y.S.3d [illegible] (App. Div. 2021) (on the [illegible] of labor arbitration for statutory discrimination claims).

B. THE DUTY TO BARGAIN DURING THE TERM OF AN EXISTING AGREEMENT

Page 916. Add to Problems for Discussion:

6. The [illegible] Company is unionized. Its collective agreement sets out a [illegible] that reserves to the Company the power to issue all [illegible] necessary to [illegible] efficient and safe production and delivery of its products; that all members of the bargaining unit will be bound to observe the terms of the Employee Handbook. The Handbook [illegible] provides that, "In the event of any accident involving physical injury or damage in excess of $[illegible], a check on the driver's driving history [illegible] and all moving violations will be made."

The collective agreement expired on December [illegible]. The parties are in the process of negotiating a new collective agreement. On January [illegible], the Company announced that as of January [illegible], checks on driving history will be made annually for each driver. The union has filed a charge of violation of Section 8(a)(5). The Company has responded that the change was consistent with the [illegible] of management rights. Should the General Counsel issue a complaint? [illegible] (D.C. Cir. 2021).

PART SIX

SUCCESSORSHIP

Page 939. Add at end of Problem for Discussion:

2. The Rosemont company has acquired a nursing home whose employees are unionized and are governing by a current collective bargaining agreement. Rosemont has invited the current workforce to apply for jobs. Sixty-four did so and were interviewed. During the interviews four Rosemont workers were asked if they were union members. They stated truthfully that they were; the four were hired. Meanwhile applicants who had not worked at the facility were also interviewed. On the first day of work under Rosemont management the staff consisted of 101 workers: 49 had previously worked at the facility, 52 had not. Was it an unfair labor practice for Rosemont to have asked if the applicants were union members? Must Rosemont bargain with the union? Ridgewood Health Care Center, Inc. v. NLRB, 8 F.4th 1263 (11th Cir. 2021).

In *UGL-UNICCO Service Co.*, 357 NLRB 801 (2011), the Board found its recognition bar rule to apply to the situation of a union becoming a bargaining representative by virtue of successorship. The Board reaffirmed that doctrine by vote of 2–1 over a lengthy dissent by member Ring. Hospital Menonita de Guyama, Inc., 371 NLRB No. 108 (2022).

PART EIGHT

FEDERALISM AND LABOR RELATIONS

I. PREEMPTION OF STATE LABOR LAW: AN OVERVIEW

Page 1012. Add at end of Problem 8:

As the Supplement goes to press, the New York legislature enacted a similar law. Chris Mare, *New York Bar on 'Captive Audience' Meetings Sent to Gov. Hochul*, BLOOMBERG LAW NEWS (June 16, 2023).

Page 1013. Add to Problems for Discussion:

10. The State regulates the provision of home health services: home care aides must meet certain educational and training requirements and be state certified; a list of certified home care aides is maintained by the Department of Health; entities providing home health services are required to hire only state-certified home care aides.

The States has amended its Health and Safety Code by adding Section 1792:

(1) The Department shall provide an electronic copy of a registered home care aide's name, telephone number, and cellular telephone number on file with the department, upon its request, to a labor organization which exists for the purpose, in whole or in part, of dealing with employers of home care aides concerning access to training, grievances, labor disputes, wages, rates of pay, hours of employment, or conditions of work. The labor organization shall not use this information of any purpose other than employee organizing, representation, and assistance activities. The labor organization shall not disclose this information to any other party.

(2) The department shall establish a simple opt-out procedure by which a registered home care aide or registered home care aide applicant may request that his or her contact information on file with the department not be disclosed in response to a request described in paragraph (1).

Suit has been brought by the Home Care Association (HCA), an association of for-profit employers providing home health services, against the state to enjoin the law on grounds of preemption by the National Labor Relations Act. The HCA has been held to have standing. Is the law preempted? Home Care Ass'n v. Newsom, 525 F. Supp. 3d 1128 (E.D. Cal. 2020).

Page 1015. Add to the end of Problem 3:

Google maintains a confidentiality policy binding on its employees and supervisors that bears on what they may say to competitors, to public agencies or outside parties, or to one another. Insofar as speech covered by § 7 is concerned Google agreed to a settle an unfair labor practice charge by posting a notice informing employees of their § 7 rights. Nevertheless, the policy was challenged as in violation of California's constitutional right of free speech that binds private entities as well as government. Doe v. Google, Inc., 268 Cal.Rptr.3d 783 (2020). For more on "local interest" see *Glacier Northwest, Inc. v. Teamsters No. 174*, 475 P.3d 1025 (Wash. App. 2020), *rev. granted*, 483 P.3d 771 (Wash. 2021).

Is New York's Farm Laborers Fair Labor Practice Law preempted? N.Y.S. Vegetable Growers Ass'n, Inc. v. Cuomo, 474 F.Supp.3d 572 (S.D.N.Y. 2020).

Page 1015. Add after Problems for Discussion:

Glacier Northwest, Inc. v. Teamsters Local No. 174

143 S. Ct.1404 (2023).

[■ JUSTICE BARRETT delivered the opinion of the Court.]

* * *

We relay the facts as alleged in the complaint. Glacier Northwest sells ready-mix concrete to customers in Washington State. Each batch must be mixed to the customer's specifications. After Glacier combines the raw ingredients—cement, sand, aggregate, admixture, and water—in a hopper, it transfers the resulting concrete to one of its trucks for prompt delivery.

In this business, time is of the essence. Concrete is highly perishable—it begins to harden immediately once at rest. Ready-mix trucks can preserve concrete in a rotating drum located on the back of the truck, but only for a limited time. If concrete remains in the rotating drum for too long, it will harden and cause significant damage to the truck. Worse still, the hardening begins right away if the drum stops revolving.

The International Brotherhood of Teamsters Local Union No. 174 (Union) serves as the exclusive bargaining representative for Glacier's truck drivers. After the collective-bargaining agreement between Glacier and the Union expired in the summer of 2017, the parties negotiated in an attempt to reach a new deal. Things did not go smoothly.

Tensions came to a head on the morning of August 11. According to the allegations in Glacier's complaint, a Union agent signaled for a work stoppage when the Union knew that Glacier was in the midst of mixing substantial amounts of concrete, loading batches into ready-mix trucks, and making deliveries. Although Glacier quickly instructed drivers to finish deliveries in progress, the Union directed them to ignore Glacier's orders. At least 16 drivers who had already set out for deliveries returned with fully loaded trucks. Seven parked their trucks, notified a Glacier representative, and either asked for instructions or took actions to protect their trucks. But at least nine drivers abandoned their trucks without a word to anyone.

Glacier faced an emergency. The company could not leave the mixed concrete in the trucks because the concrete's inevitable hardening would cause significant damage to the vehicles. At the same time, the company could not dump the concrete out of the trucks at random because concrete contains environmentally sensitive chemicals. To top it all off, Glacier had limited time to solve this conundrum.

A mad scramble ensued. Glacier needed to determine which trucks had concrete in them, how close the concrete in each truck was to hardening, and where to dump that concrete in an environmentally safe manner. Over the course of five hours, nonstriking employees built special bunkers and managed to offload the concrete. When all was said and done, Glacier's emergency maneuvers prevented damage to its trucks. But the concrete that it had already mixed that day hardened in the bunkers and became useless.

Glacier sued the Union for damages in Washington state court. Relying on the allegations detailed above, Glacier claimed that the Union intentionally destroyed the company's concrete and that this conduct amounted to common law conversion and trespass to chattels.

The Union moved to dismiss Glacier's tort claims on the ground that the NLRA preempted them. In the Union's view, the NLRA at least arguably protected the drivers' conduct, so the State was powerless to hold the Union accountable for any of the strike's consequences.

[The Supreme Court of Washington held the lawsuit to be preempted under *Garmon*. The U.S. Supreme Court granted certiorari.]

* * *

As the party asserting preemption, the Union bears the burden of (1) advancing "an interpretation of the [NLRA] that is not plainly contrary to its language and that has not been 'authoritatively rejected' by the courts or the Board," and then (2) putting forth "enough evidence to enable the court to find that" the NLRA arguably protects the drivers' conduct. [Longshoremen v. Davis, 476 U.S. 380, 395 (1986).] The Union passes the first test but fails the second.

All agree that the NLRA protects the right to strike but that this right is not absolute. . . . The Board has long taken the position—which both the Union and Glacier accept—that the NLRA does not shield strikers who fail to take "reasonable precautions" to protect their employer's property from foreseeable, aggravated, and imminent danger due to the sudden cessation of work. *Bethany Medical Center*, 328 N.L.R.B. 1094 (1999) ("concerted activity" is "indefensible where employees fail to take reasonable precautions to protect the employer's plant, equipment, or products from foreseeable imminent danger due to sudden cessation of work"). . . . Given this undisputed limitation on the right to strike, we proceed to consider whether the Union has demonstrated that the statute arguably protects the drivers' conduct. . . .

The drivers engaged in a sudden cessation of work that put Glacier's property in foreseeable and imminent danger. The Union knew that concrete is highly perishable and that it can last for only a limited time in a delivery truck's rotating drum. It also knew that concrete left to harden in a truck's drum causes significant damage to the truck. The Union nevertheless coordinated with truck drivers to initiate the strike when Glacier was in the midst of batching large quantities of concrete and delivering it to customers. Predictably, the company's concrete was destroyed as a result. And though Glacier's swift action saved its trucks in the end, the risk of harm to its equipment was both foreseeable and serious. *See NLRB* v. *Special Touch Home Care Services, Inc.*, 708 F. 3d 447, 460 (CA2 2013) ("The appropriate inquiry is focused on the *risk* of harm, not its realization").

The Union failed to "take reasonable precautions to protect" against this foreseeable and imminent danger. *Bethany Medical Center,* 328 N. L. R. B., at 1094. It could have initiated the strike before Glacier's trucks were full of wet concrete—say, by instructing drivers to refuse to load their trucks in the first place. Once the strike was underway, nine of the Union's drivers abandoned their fully loaded trucks without telling anyone—which left the trucks on a path to destruction unless Glacier saw them in time to unload the concrete. Yet the Union did not take the simple step of alerting Glacier that these trucks had been returned. Nor, after the trucks were in the yard, did the Union direct its drivers to follow Glacier's instructions to facilitate a safe transfer of equipment. To be clear, the "reasonable precautions" test does not mandate any one action in particular. But the Union's failure to take even minimal precautions illustrates its failure to fulfill its duty.

Indeed, far from taking reasonable precautions to mitigate foreseeable danger to Glacier's property, the Union executed the strike in a manner designed to compromise the safety of Glacier's trucks and destroy its concrete. Such conduct is not "arguably protected" by the NLRA; on the contrary, it goes well beyond the NLRA's protections. See *NLRB* v. *Marshall Car Wheel & Foundry Co.*, 218 F. 2d 409, 411, 413 (CA5 1955) (strike unprotected when employees abandoned their posts without warning "when molten iron in the plant cupola was ready to be poured off," even though "a lack of sufficient help to carry out the critical pouring operation might well have resulted in substantial property damage").

Thus, accepting the complaint's allegations as true, the Union did not take reasonable precautions to protect Glacier's property from imminent danger resulting from the drivers' sudden cessation of work.

The state court thus erred in dismissing Glacier's tort claims as preempted on the pleadings.

[The Court went on to distinguish cases that held protected strikes that resulted in the loss of perishable food then being processed as the drivers *"prompted the creation of the perishable product"* (italics in original). It opined that while the decision "to initiate the strike during the workday and failure to give Glacier specific notice do not themselves render its conduct unprotected" that conduct is relevant in evaluating "whether strikers took reasonable precautions, whether harm to property was imminent, and whether that danger was foreseeable." It discounted the Union's claim that care had been taken to keep the drums rotating as inadequately supported.

At the close the Court adds this footnote:

> After the Washington Supreme Court affirmed the dismissal of Glacier's tort claims, the Board's general counsel issued a complaint alleging that Glacier engaged in unfair labor practices in relation to its labor dispute with the drivers, including by disciplining some of those involved in the strike. The lower courts have not addressed the significance, if any, of the Board's complaint with respect to *Garmon* preemption. We will not do so in the first instance. *Cutter* v. *Wilkinson*, 544 U.S. 709, 718, n. 7 (2005) ("[W]e are a court of review, not of first view"). The Board's general counsel agrees that this issue is not properly before us. See Brief for United States as *Amicus Curiae* 28.]

* * *

[■ JUSTICE THOMAS, with whom JUSTICE GORSUCH joined, concurred in the judgment but found the *Garmon* approach atypical and "strange."]

The majority opinion today underscores the strangeness of the *Garmon* regime. Here, the Supreme Court of the United States reassures a state court of its power to adjudicate a state-law tort claim. The Court does so, not based on its own judgment that federal law does not pre-empt the claim, but because the NLRB's existing precedents adequately remove any "[c]lou[d]" over the matter. 359 U. S., at 246. But, if the Board's precedents left the matter "arguable" (and the NLRA did not plainly dictate an answer), then the state courts would be "ousted" of jurisdiction. *Longshoremen* v. *Davis*, 476 U. S. 380, 396 (1986). The upshot of this approach appears to be that the scope of the NLRA's pre-emption of state-court jurisdiction over state claims is defined—not by the statutory text—but by "penumbra[s]" that wax and wane as the Board develops, or declines to develop, its own carefully insulated common law of labor relations. *Garmon*, 359 U. S., at 240 (internal quotation marks omitted).

The parties here have not asked us to reconsider *Garmon*, nor is it necessary to do so to resolve this case. Nonetheless, in an appropriate case, we should carefully reexamine whether the law supports *Garmon*'s "unusual" pre-emption regime.

* * *

[■ JUSTICE ALITO, joined by JUSTICES THOMAS and GORSUCH, concurred in the judgment pointing to the *Fansteel* case of 1939 and others as standing for the categorical proposition that the destruction of property is not protected by the Labor Act: "Nothing more is needed to resolve the case." They addressed Justice Jackson's dissent, alluded to but not mentioned in the footnote in the majority's opinion set out above. Their address to it will be taken up after the dissent is treated.]

* * *

[■ JUSTICE JACKSON dissented, and at length. She echoed the majority's recital of the two-step test for *Garmon* preemption, with this prefatory caution.]

But the term "preemption" is something of a misnomer. Rather than entirely and automatically precluding the state-court suit, the rule instead requires state courts to take a "jurisdictional hiatus" while the Board considers the dispute in the first instance. . . . If the Board determines (subject to judicial review) that § 7 protects the union's conduct, normal conflict preemption kicks in: A state court may not hold a union liable on state-law claims for conduct that is protected by the NLRA. See *Brown* v. *Hotel Employees*, 468 U. S. 491, 503 (1984). But "if the Board decides that the conduct is not protected," the state court may proceed to "entertain the litigation." *Davis*, 476 U. S., at 397.[1]

* * *

[Justice Jackson then turned to what the majority's footnote, quoted above, treated as not before the Court.]

The filing of the General Counsel's administrative complaint necessarily suffices to establish that the Union's strike conduct is "arguably protected" within the meaning of *Garmon*. Thus, the General Counsel's complaint should have marked the end of any court involvement in this matter at this time.

The General Counsel's complaint alleges that Glacier interfered with strike conduct protected by § 7 when it disciplined its drivers for walking off the job and when it filed this tort suit. That complaint represents the General Counsel's conclusion—reached after an extensive independent investigation involving collecting testimony and other evidence, and after

---

1 JUSTICE THOMAS seeks to undercut our *Garmon* precedent by describing it as "od[d]" and "strang[e]" relative to " 'the usual preemption rule.' ". . . But, as discussed, the *Garmon* rule is not a standard preemption doctrine; it is different because it is doing different work. *Garmon* protects Congress's judgment that the Board, not state or federal courts, should be generally responsible for the development of our Nation's labor law. The required pause when *Garmon*'s "arguably protected" test is satisfied allows for efficient resolution of the dispute prior to the expenditure of state judicial resources, and the temporary nature of the pause makes it narrower, not broader, in effect than ordinary preemption.

careful consideration of the competing legal principles and policy concerns—that the Union's claim that its strike conduct was protected "appears to have merit." 29 CFR §§ 101.4, 101.8. One "cannot credibly contend that a claim that makes it through this gauntlet does not concern conduct 'arguably' protected by the NLRA." *Davis Supermarkets, Inc.* v. *NLRB*, 2 F. 3d 1162, 1179 (CADC 1993); accord, *Makro, Inc.*, 305 N.L.R.B. 663, 670 (1991).

A court presented with a General Counsel complaint should therefore find *Garmon* inherently satisfied. This is so because the entire point of *Garmon*'s arguably-protected test is to permit the court to assess the facts and relevant labor law in service of a *gatekeeping* function. The answer to the *Garmon* question simply (and solely) establishes whether the court can continue to entertain a lawsuit that relates to the challenged strike conduct, or whether the le- gal action must be suspended to allow the Board to make an initial assessment of the matter. The court evaluates the existing evidence and the law for a specific reason: to determine whether the lawsuit attacks arguably-protected conduct such that entertaining the legal action will inter- fere with the Board's prerogative to develop the facts and adjudicate the merits of the dispute as part of the Board's broader authority to develop national labor law.

If the General Counsel investigates the matter and files a complaint with the Board alleging that the union's conduct is protected, it becomes indisputable that the pending legal action might interfere with the Board's authority. Thus, a General Counsel complaint relieves the court of the burden of having to make the arguably-protected assessment based on its *own* understanding of the evidence and labor law—it is "arguable" that the union's conduct is protected because the General Counsel is arguing just that. To be sure, we have said that the arguably-protected test is "not without substance" and is "not satisfied by a conclusory assertion of pre-emption." *Davis*, 476 U. S., at 394. But an allegation from the Board's General Counsel after a thorough investigation is a far cry from a "conclusory assertion" of protection.[2]

* * *

[Justice Jackson then addressed the majority's reason for declining to consider the fact that the General Counsel issued a complaint, which was in process of being heard by an Administrative Law Judge.]

[The majority's] rationale is inconsistent with the broader approach that the majority takes in this case. It would be one thing if the Court simply noted the filing of the General Counsel's complaint and authorized the lower courts to evaluate the impact of that complaint on the *Garmon* question in the first instance. But it goes further: The

---

[2] This is not to suggest that the General Counsel's complaint is the end of the story, as the Board may ultimately disagree with the factual or legal basis of that pleading. But the complaint is surely sufficient to establish *arguable* protection, such that a court should stay its hand.

majority also inserts itself into the midst of this labor dispute *now* (despite the General Counsel's complaint), proceeding to apply the Board's cases to novel and difficult line-drawing questions and ultimately concluding that the strike conduct alleged in Glacier's complaint is not even arguably protected.

The majority cannot have it both ways. A concern about the Court's institutional role justifies, at most, vacating the judgment below and remanding for the lower court to con- sider the import of the General Counsel's complaint. The same observation that compels the majority to allow for such lower-court consideration—that we are " 'a court of review, not of first view,' ". . .—should have likewise led it to decline to intrude into this labor dispute while it is pending before the Board.

* * *

[In the next part of her opinion Justice Jackson separately addressed the fact specific and, as she saw it, highly nuanced question of what a union's obligations to the employer are in a strike situation and, again, of the Labor Board's role of striking the balance in the first instance. She then dwelt on how the union's conduct could be squared with Board precedent; that the risk that concrete would harden in the trucks "involves a relatively complex factual analysis under the Board's reasonable-precautions principles". She emphasized the distinction that, she says, Justice Alito elided, between "affirmative steps of violence or property seizure" and "peacefully stopping work (and the economic consequences that flow from that decision)."]

* * *

Justice Alito addressed the dissent in this footnote:

The Court wisely declines to address the argument on which JUSTICE JACKSON relies regarding the effect of the complaint before the NLRB on this litigation. . . . That argument represents a striking extension of *Garmon* preemption, which, as the Court notes, is already an "unusual" doctrine. . . . If the state courts on remand dismiss this case on that ground, the decision, in my judgment, would be a good candidate for a quick return trip here.

* * *

QUESTIONS FOR DISCUSSION

1. As the casebook points out, *Garmon* has long been characterized as resting on a "primary jurisdiction" ground of preemption. Primary jurisdiction is a doctrine in federal administrative law that speaks to the situation of a state action brought, for example, in tort or contract and for which there is no question of the state court's jurisdiction to hear, but that nevertheless has a connection to or a bearing on a federal scheme such that the state court's proceeding might upset or wrongly impinge on that scheme. The doctrine requires the state court to hold the case in abeyance whilst resort is had to the federal agency with jurisdiction over the scheme to see if such interference is so. Justice Jackson calls this "a *Garmon* hiatus." In what way is *Garmon* "unusual" or "strange"?

2. The majority points to *Garmon's* ground for the state to stay its hand even when resort to Board's General Counsel has not been made or where the General Counsel declined to act. In the case, however, resort was had, a complaint issued and was in the process of being heard. Is it now open to the Washington state court on remand to stay the case pending the Board's disposition—or that disposition's fate before a Court of Appeals?

3. Justice Jackson thinks the rule should be this: the General Counsel's issuance of a complaint asserting that an employer's discipline of strikers for their strike activity should satisfy the requirement of arguability so to trigger the "*Garmon* hiatus." The majority declines to address her proposal, but three Justices vehemently disagree. What would be wrong, legally or practically, with that rule from the perspective of the policy undergirding *Garmon* preemption?

4. Gogol Pharmaceuticals makes a variety of products: some are produced in continuous lines of production on a 24/7 schedule; others are produced in batches taking 10 to 18 hours to complete. All production is controlled and monitored by computers whose operatives are highly trained. They, and the warehouse employees who stock and transport the raw materials into the plant and stock and transport the finished products out of it, are represented by the Pharmaceutical Workers Union. Some of the raw materials are highly perishable: they arrive on a "just in time" basis and must be stored safely and processed quickly. So, too, some of the finished products require special storage in controlled cold conditions.

The Union and the Company have been bargaining for months over wages and work scheduling, especially overtime for batch work. On November 1, the membership authorized the Union's executive committee to call a strike "at such time as they see fit". Management was notified of the vote. The parties agreed to bargain starting November 10 on a "marathon" basis to see if an agreement could be made. At 4:30 am on November 11 the bargaining concluded with no agreement and with none in prospect. The union's executive committee met at 5:30 am to decide when to strike. You are the Union's lawyer. The executive committee has asked you if they can call to strike to begin at 8:00 that morning, at the shift change for workers in continuous production, batch workers being scheduled according to the schedules for batch processing time. What advice would you give?

II. SPECIFIC APPLICATIONS: REPRESENTATION, BARGAINING AND CONCERTED ACTIVITIES

B. COLLECTIVE BARGAINING

Page 1044. Add at end of Problem 6:

See also Columbia Sussex Mgmt., LLC v. City of Santa Monica, 482 F. Supp. 3d 1002 (C.D. Cal. 2020).

Page 1045. Add new Problem:

10. New York has adopted a law "in relation to occupational exposure to an airborne infectious disease." It requires the adoption of health standards and the creation of joint employer-employee workplace health and safety committees. N.Y. Lab. L. § 27–d (2021): "Employers shall permit employees to establish and administer a joint labor-management workplace safety committee" to be composed of employee and employer designees. Where there is a union the latter will be designated by the union. The committee is to be co-chaired by an employer representative and a representative of non-supervisory employees. Is this requirement preempted by § 8(a)(2)? On similar enactments see Matthew Finkin, *Employee Representation Outside the Labor Act: Thoughts on Arbitral Representation, Group Arbitrations, and Workplace Committees*, 5 U. PA. J. LAB. & EMP. L. 75 (2002) ("group arbitration" now truncated by *Epic Systems*, casebook page 552).

C. ENFORCEMENT OF COLLECTIVE AGREEMENTS

Page 1068. Add at the end of the second paragraph in Problem 5:

Compare Melendez v. San Francisco Baseball Associates, LLC, 439 P.3d 764 (Cal. 2010) (wage payment laws not § 301 preempted).

Page 1068. Add to Problems for Discussion:

6. Illinois' Biometric Privacy Information Act, 740 ILCS 14/1 et seq., regulates the acquisition and use of biometric information, such as fingerprints, by employers. The employer must:

> (1) inform[s] the subject or the subject's legally authorized representative in writing that a biometric identifier or biometric information is being collected or stored;
>
> (2) inform[s] the subject or the subject's legally authorized representative in writing of the specific purpose and length of term for which a biometric identifier or biometric information is being collected, stored, and used; and
>
> (3) receive[s] a written release executed by the subject of the biometric identifier or biometric information or the subject's legally authorized representative.

The Major Container Company has a collective agreement with the Paperworks Union governing the employees in Chicago, Illinois, identical to the one out the recognition clause (Art. II) in its collective bargaining agreement on page 107 of the Supplement. The Company has instituted a new timekeeping system that requires employees to press their thumbs on an electronic plate that records their fingerprint in order to enter and leave the faculty. None were asked to sign a written release.

Wally Cox is a Major Container production worker in Chicago. He has brought a class action on behalf of all Chicago employees—production, maintenance, and office clerical personnel—for violation of BIPA. The Company has moved to dismiss on grounds of Section 301 pre-emption. How should the court rule? Fernandez v. Kerry, Inc., 14 F.4th 644 (7th Cir. 2021),